Higher Education Policy Series 44

Lifelong Learning
The Politics of the New Learning Environment
Geoffrey Elliott

Jessica Kingsley Publishers
London and Philadelphia

The right of Geoffrey Elliott to be identified as author of this work has been asserted by him in accordance with the Copyright, Designs and Patents Act 1988.

First published in the United Kingdom in 1999 by
Jessica Kingsley Publishers Ltd
116 Pentonville Road,
London N1 9JB
and
325 Chestnut Street,
Philadelphia, PA 19106, USA

www.jkp.com

Library of Congress Cataloging in Publication Data

A CIP catalogue record for this book is available from the Library of Congress

British Library Cataloguing in Publication Data
Elliott, Geoff
Lifelong learning : the politics of the new learning environment.
- (Higher education policy; 44)
1. Learning 2. Education, Higher - Aims and objectives
I. Title
370.1'523

ISBN 1 85302 580 1

Printed and Bound in Great Britain by
Athenaeum Press, Gateshead, Tyne and Wear

Contents

List of figures   6

Acknowledgements   6

1   What's going on?   7

2   Sources, courses and educational discourses   17

3   Lifelong learning what?   29

4   'Before I never looked in the back'   47

5   'I'm a me'   63

6   Darkness visible, or research in post-compulsory education   79

7   Education, education, education reports   93

8   A very long and heavy document   111

References   133

Subject index   141

Author index   143

List of Figures

Figure 5.1   Cross-cutting themes in student learning   76
Figure 5.2   Levels of analysis of student learning   77
Figure 7.1   The Dearing qualifications framework for   101
             higher education

Acknowledgements

I owe thanks to my family for love and support; Charles A Elliott F.L.A. for preparing the indexes; the Policy into Practice Research Centre, University College Worcester for financial assistance with the interview study; Jackie Pratchett for invaluable advice, insight and help with the student interviews; the FE Colleges and tutors who kindly agreed to take part; and the students for their wholehearted engagement with the project.

CHAPTER ONE

What's Going On?

This book is about learning in post-compulsory education, but it has a broader purpose which is to reclaim lifelong learning as a socio-political project in which universities and colleges can play a key part. So too can pre-school groups, schools, libraries, employers and others with responsibilities within the social and economic fabric of society. However, while I can acknowledge their role in bringing about a society of lifelong learning, I must leave to others the task of expanding upon it. My concern is to move the debate about what happens in universities and colleges closer to those the system is there to provide for, namely the students.

Those whose learning experiences are presented in this book are following or have recently followed access or foundation year zero courses in further education (FE) colleges. They are thus all regarded within the system as mature students, and most entered their course without formal qualifications. Martin Trow has suggested that the central question for a system of mass higher education (HE) is 'what's going on?' (1997, p.26). By its exploration of the concerns of students who stand at the interface between the two sectors which comprise the post-compulsory education system in the UK, this book is an attempt to contribute an answer. Trow's criticism of the National Committee of Inquiry into Higher Education (NCIHE), the Dearing Report (NCIHE 1997), is that it attempts to answer a different question: 'what should we do?', which is one that should more properly be asked of colleges and universities in an élite system. The consequence of asking the wrong questions is one of the themes of this book, since it argues that educational research has consistently failed to address the interests of students and staff as a consequence of an over-formalised conception of education and an over-socialised view of education systems. For the Dearing Committee, the consequence is a missed opportunity to reflect the needs and concerns of those working as students and teachers in the university sector and to link those concerns to those of their counterparts in further education. As Trow notes:

> There is an extraordinary amount of exhortation to staff to do more with less, but very little feeling of academic life as students and teachers live and experience it, and little sense of the enormous variety in that experience ... This report, in those large sections that address the private life of higher education, the life of teaching and learning, simply does not know what is going on inside the colleges and universities, their classrooms and offices and laboratories, but still pronounces with an air of great authority about what should be happening. (Trow 1997, p.26)

The Dearing Report was a much awaited document, the first major government review of higher education since the Robbins Committee (1962) looked forward to a continuing expansion of an élite higher education system over 30 years earlier. The report has had a mixed reception but no criticism as penetrating as Trow's, which strikes at the heart of the purposes of the report and raises important doubts about many of the recommendations that it makes to government, funding and quality bodies, institutions, and individual academics.

One of the prevailing othodoxies that the report does go some way to correcting is that students' learning is now framed within a 'new learning environment' (NCIHE 1997, pp.36, 119). Against the concerns of some that new technology is being used in further and higher education as a cost-driven way of replacing staff:student contact time thereby increasing the staff:student ratio, need to be set the claims of others who are sceptical because they hold fast to a luddite resistance to IT, and yet others who remain genuinely fearful about the future of their own professional role in the face of changes that herald a more technological, student-driven learning environment. It is one of the key assertions of this book that the linkages between learning, teaching and the technology that supports the concept of the new learning environment must be properly understood if effective learning and teaching strategies for the millenium are to be developed. This claim is supported by one of the gurus of new information technology, Bill Gates of Microsoft:

> Billionaire US software magnate Bill Gates warned this week
> that the Government's plans for a computer-based National
> Grid for Learning would be fruitless unless teachers were given
> proper training in information technology ... Microsoft [plans]
> to set up a teacher resource centre, an on-line teacher training
> network, in collaboration with BT and RM plc. 'Technology
> can't be a substitute for a good teacher,' he said. 'It is just a tool in
> the hands of teachers'. (*The Times Higher Educational Supplement*
> (THES) 1997a, p.2)

The central place that teachers play in facilitating learning through
new technologies has been recognised within the further education
sector:

> Colleges now have a substantial amount of modern information
> technology equipment and the technological infrastructure
> needed to develop effective support for learning. The develop-
> ment of well-equipped learning resource centres, often associ-
> ated with libraries, has been a notable characteristic of recent
> college activity. Students generally have good access to informa-
> tion technology, although there remain some colleges which do
> not have sufficient, modern resources. It is now a priority for the
> sector to develop a better understanding of how to use informa-
> tion technology most effectively in the curriculum to ensure that
> students develop appropriate key skills in relation to its use. The
> potential for information technology to increase the breadth of
> students' learning and experience is substantial. However, teach-
> ers need support if this potential is to be realised. (Further Edu-
> cation Council (FEFC) 1997a, p.5)

Although the discourse of wiring up Britain and the virtual campus is
a familiar one, it is less certain how far institutions and those who
work in them have moved or are prepared to move towards the
establishment of a new learning environment. It is also apparent that
the new technology which is at the heart of the new learning
environment does not come without a price. At the time of writing
much media scorn was being poured on one new university following
a major technical breakdown of its new multi-million pound learning
resource centre. More significant though are residual concerns about
the social, cultural and economic impact of the technology – how it is
used, by whom, and to what end. The Higginson Committee Report
(FEFC 1996), which looked at new technologies in further

education, identified a large number of leading edge installations and applications. However, if we look at what's going on, the picture is one of not quite so brave a new world:

> Whilst the new technologies hold the prospect of encouraging new ways of learning, imaginative interchange at a distance, and access to unimaginable riches of information, they also exclude. Whatever the potential of the Internet for the dispossessed, it is affluent young men in urban environments who are its major users. (National Institute for Adult Continuing Education (NIACE) 1997, p.9)

Similarly, the FEFC has noted the need to 'develop and disseminate good practice and alleviate the unevenness which characterises the use of information technology in many colleges and across the sector, as a whole' (FEFC 1997a, p. 5).

There is also a continuing need to recall the diversity of the student body, particularly, but by no means exclusively, the mature student group which forms the focus of this book. The importance of this is recognised in a DfEE briefing paper, *Getting the Most out of HE – Supporting Learner Autonomy* which notes that mature students 'have particular needs, arising from external commitments, to employers and families, which constrain how they can receive guidance, and how they can interact with the institution, though as more students take on paid employment in term time this issue may become more widespread' (Department for Education and Employment 1997, p.20).

The starting point for thinking about a new learning environment is best determined by asking the naive question 'what is new?' The emphasis on environment suggests that the physical attributes of the learning context may be new, and indeed many recent funded learning projects are heavily reliant upon new technology to create a new set of assumptions about how students will learn. Notable examples are the Effective Learning Programme at the University of Lincolnshire and Humberside, sponsored by BP, and the STILE (Students' and Teachers' Integrated Learning Environment) Project at the Universities of Leicester, Loughborough, De Montfort and the Open University, sponsored by the four UK higher education funding bodies.

However effective such projects may be, debates about new forms of learning that do not take account of previous forms may have the charge of vacuousness levelled against them. The key importance of the context of learning is illustrated in organisational contexts by the work of Argyris and Schon (1978), who developed Bateson's (1973) concept of deutero-learning; the point applies equally to other contexts as well:

> When an organisation engages in deutero-learning, its members learn too about previous contexts for learning. They reflect on and enquire into previous episodes of organisational learning or failure to learn. They discover what they did that facilitated or in-hibited learning, they invent new strategies for learning, and they evaluate and generalise what they have produced. The results be-come encoded in individual maps and are reflected in organisa-tional learning practice. (Argyris and Schon 1978, p.186)

The essence of deutero-learning is when learners engage in what Brookfield describes as 'discussing and reflecting upon their own learning styles' (1986, p.192); he also highlights the importance of the linked concept of mathetics, or how adults learn how to learn:

> R. M. Smith, for example, has spent the last two decades devel-oping a theory and practical repertoire of training exercises premised on the idea that it is as important to teach adults how to learn as it is to specify particular curricular domains for learning. He advocates that educators become sensitive to this idea and in-clude a 'learning-how-to-learn' orientation for new instructors and learners at the outset of a program, so that they can use their newly acquired awareness of their own learning styles to gain as much insight, knowlege and analytical capacity from the subse-quent course as possible (Smith and Havercamp 1977). (Brook-field 1986, p.64)

This serves as an important reminder that it is not sufficient to attempt to create a new learning environment without giving careful thought to how it will impact positively or negatively upon students, teachers and the learning process.

In an influential study of university teaching, Laurillard 'starts from the premise that university teachers must take the main responsibility for what and how their students learn' (1993, p.1). This is an important statement of the university teacher's professional responsibility, and contrasts starkly with the reality of 'impersonal departments whose staff have never taken a great deal of interest in the learning process, whose students are "at arm's length", lacking an

understanding of course goals and assessment and with little control
over the pace of work ...' (McIlroy 1994, p.35). Few would dispute in
which setting student learning development will be stifled rather than
fostered, however Laurillard proceeds to argue that 'academic
learning is different from other kinds of learning in everyday life
because it is not directly experienced, and is necessarily mediated by
the teacher' (1993, p.5). According to this view the student is not
learning about the world directly but about the descriptions of the
world held by the teachers of her academic courses whose role is cast
as one of mediator. The problem with this is quite clear. It takes the
statement made by Ramsden which is cited by Laurillard with
approval: 'The aim of teaching is simple: it is to make student learning
possible' (Ramsden 1992, p.5), and proposes the logical *non sequitur*
that if all teaching is designed to make student learning possible, then
no learning can take place without teaching, which is self-evidently
not the case. Students in universities learn from technicians,
librarians and other support staff; they learn from their own experience of the world gained directly by reading, experimenting,
painting, browsing the Internet, attending performances,
experiencing field trips, thinking and reflecting, engaging in
conversation and discussion, making connections between different
and separate experiences, and so on. All of these learning moments
are direct in that they are instances of the student interacting with the
real world of which teachers and what they say are also a significant
part. Privileging teaching contexts over other forms of learning
experience is a consequence of a formalised view of education that
understates the extent to which students may take responsibility for
their own learning and equally how much of that learning may take
place outside of formal academic contexts.

Laurillard presents a clear and attractive model for university
teaching which emphasises the importance for teachers of taking into
account common miscomprehensions by students about the subject
and topic when designing teaching and learning materials. However,
the danger of a model of student learning that minimises the extent to
which learning takes place outside of formal academic contexts is that
of over-reliance upon pedagogic strategies such as described by
Laurillard to foster deep approaches to learning (Biggs 1982), and a
failure to recognise that a broader engagement on the part of teachers
with the whole range of the student experience is necessary in order to

understand why sometimes well designed teaching strategies appear to fail and less well thought out approaches may succeed. It is important not to overstate the case for the centrality of university teaching since the new learning environment may simply not allow for the customarily substantial extent of teacher–student contact that is still found in some undergraduate programmes.

It is an argument of this book that the teacher's role is one of supporting student learning and that that role is best carried out by directing the student's attention to *how* they learn in different contexts and when faced with different learning tasks. It is neither helpful nor congruent with commonplace practices to construct academic learning as a separate and distinct category of learning task. Such a construction simply perpetuates the practice of seeing university teaching as a process which transmits pearls of wisdom from old scholars to new apprentices. This is a long way from conceiving of student learning as the vivid and everyday experience of creating an awareness that there is a variety of perspectives, a number of ways of seeing, that we inhabit different and multiple worlds, and that academic knowledge is accessible and useful for its capacity to broaden our focus. None of these things is possible if academic learning is something that needs to be 'mediated', as if this knowledge is something other than a living and urgent set of understandings about the world and the social constructions of it that are lived out in universities and elsewhere. My analysis deliberately moves away from what Laurillard calls 'the second-order character of academic knowledge' (1993, p.94). What is at issue is not that academic knowledge consists of second-order propositions, but rather that it is in this respect in any way different in kind from other propositions which should to an equal extent be viewed as instances of situated and context-specific discourse which needs to be deconstructed or 'read' by participants.

It is precisely because it is not possible to specify what students will learn in terms of what teachers teach that the use of the term 'learning outcome' is gaining in popularity as a way of describing what it is that academic courses do. Curriculum planning needs to begin at the point of describing what students learn, not what teachers teach. This is not to marginalise teachers but simply to put in proper perspective the part that both teachers and learners play in the process. As Allan puts it, 'the process of defining and expressing learning outcomes should enable lecturers to reflect upon what they intend their students to learn and thereby articulate the relationship between what they teach and what students do, in fact, learn [in order] to emphasise the role of the student in accepting responsibility for his/her own learning and to acknowledge that learning might take place in a variety of settings' (Allan 1996, p.104). As teachers we must acknowledge that our part is supportive rather than dominant, constructive rather than dogmatic:

> Self-direction in learning is not a set of techniques that can be applied within a context of objectives and evaluative criteria that are determined by others. At the heart of self-directedness is the adult's assumption of control over setting educational goals and generating personally meaningful evaluative criteria. One cannot be a fully self-directed learner if one is applying techniques of independent study within a context of goals and evaluative criteria determined by an external authority. (Brookfield 1986, p.19)

An irony, however, arises from the increasing use of outcomes to define an over-prescribed curriculum, notably in vocational education and training contexts. Within NVQs, for example, the learning outcomes in use primarily reflect a piecemeal and compartmentalised conception of knowledge in which there is little room for learner autonomy, discovery in learning, and making connections across subject and discipline boundaries. The formalisation of vocational education has been widely critiqued for its mechanical interpretation of knowledge and its empty individualism (Hyland 1994; Hodkinson and Sparkes 1995; Elliott 1996).

A final word about technologies. It is important to distinguish between two senses of the word technology that are in common use in education. The first sense is technology as teaching process, where technology describes all those activities that are designed and put in place by teachers to facilitate the accomplishment of student learning. This is the broadest use of the term. The second sense is narrower and refers to what is sometimes called new technology or electronic information, and would include audio-visual media, computers, telematics and so on. All of the components of the second usage are encompassed within the first. Although potentially confusing, it is in fact helpful to retain the dual use of the term technology since it helps to avoid the temptation to think of media in isolation from other activities fundamental to learning and teaching. Many texts that promote the use of new technologies are weak in this respect, in that they adopt a reverential attitude to hardware and software without addressing the underlying issues that the use of such media presents. Some are led to make elaborate claims for the new technology and its effects on education:

> The fabric of schooling is similarly rendered obsolete by electronic networking. Everything from building design to the size, shape, alignment, and furnishing of space for the 'knowledge worker' in the school is transformed ... The concept of the virtual organization, or the learning network organization, is a reality in the knowledge society. (Caldwell 1997, p.364)

Although these directions are presented by Caldwell as a vision or *gestalt*, there is the sense that they are being flagged as the consequence of past and present occurrence. Yet the lesson of previously declared information technology revolutions is that the effects are less than dramatic when viewed on the large scale. The potential of new technology to change learning and teaching practices may be more muted that often supposed. The task then for the teachers is to begin at the starting point: how do students learn? The answers to questions of this kind can inform decisions about how far new technology can support, enhance and change what learners do. It may be helpful to distinguish between the two senses of technology by differentiating between information technology (IT) and knowledge technology. IT can refer to technological developments involving computer hardware, software, multimedia, the Internet and so on, whilst knowledge technology can refer to all the processes involved in teaching, including the use of IT. This distinction may also be helpful in reminding ourselves that information and knowledge are not one and the same, although they are often confused. What Caldwell is referring to above is an information society. A knowledge society is quite a different thing altogether.

In the next chapter a theoretical orientation for lifelong learning is proposed, and in Chapter 3 there is a critique of the prevailing orthodoxy. Chapters 4 and 5 present some interview data which reflects the experience of a group of mature students currently in post-compulsory education. There follows in Chapter 6 a discussion of methodology and Chapter 7 presents the key conclusions and issues for further and higher education arising from the three main education reports to emerge during 1997. The final chapter explores some of the deficiencies of the current policy direction and argues that a radical proactive policy approach is required to bring about a society of lifelong learning.

CHAPTER TWO

Sources, Courses and Educational Discourses

This chapter provides an overview of the book and introduces its thesis. The main themes and issues that are introduced here are very much of a contemporary nature in that they represent substantial aspects of the higher education policy debate that was launched when the Conservative government announced that a national enquiry into higher education was to be set up, chaired by Ron Dearing (NCIHE 1997). The Dearing enquiry was seen by many within and outwith higher education as a device to ensure that HE remained well and truly off of the election agenda. In this at least the enquiry was successful. As for the report itself, nationally it has had a mixed response. Some of these responses are discussed in Chapter 8. The most glaring omission in the terms of reference of the enquiry is that there is no linkage to the important enquiry into widening part-icipation in further education chaired by Helena Kennedy (FEFC 1997b), nor to the Fryer Report on lifelong learning (National Advisory Group for Continuing Education and Lifelong Learning (NAGCELL) 1997) which was intended to form the basis of a White Paper (actually to be downgraded to a Green Paper) on lifelong learning to be published in 1998. The boundaries between further and higher education are becoming increasingly blurred and in many respects a seamless progression from the former to the latter is already in place. There remain however crucial differences and disparities between the two sectors and clearly an opportunity to map out a coherent and consistent interface between them was lost. Particularly disappointing is the narrow view that is taken of the remit of further and higher education in the report and the perpetuation of boundaries between the two sectors that have no educational rationale.

The focus of this book deliberately overlaps the FE and HE boundary and the discussion of student learning is presented in the context of a group of mature students at the interface. Data is presented which has been gathered from a range of sources including open-ended interviews with mature students, observations of educational settings, a range of textual sources including current policy documents, academic studies, media responses to policy projects, and reflections upon my own practice both as a mature student and a lecturer formerly in further education and currently in higher education with a responsibility for FE/HE academic partnerships.

This is in part a study of the context of effective student learning, with a substantial focus upon courses and programmes located in FE colleges which are designed to prepare students for higher education. In recent years, a host of collaborative partnerships have built up between FE and HE, and a range of progression routes are becoming well established. Access courses which operate within the Quality Assurance Agency access recognition framework have increased in number and variety, as have foundation year courses. The proportion of HE now delivered within the FE sector has grown to eight per cent, such activity often underpinned by franchise and associate college agreements. The incorporation of both sectors has encouraged a flourishing 'market' in education, which has driven both competitive and collaborative relationships within and between the FE and university sector. The proposals under consideration by government at the time of writing for all students to pay for their education through individual lifelong learning accounts (Tysome 1997, p.3) is but one example of the marketisation of education begun by the Thatcherite force within the Conservative Party and continued by New Labour. It would appear that a new settlement has emerged which takes for granted that the market in education is now intrinsic.

In order to contextualise the book, it is important to state that data collection for the study which it reports took place during 1997–8, and the data analysis and compilation of the book took place during the few months either side of the publication of the Dearing Report. Also significant is that the graduate standards debate, which sought to identify notions of 'graduateness', was in full flow during the period of the research, as was debate on lifetime or lifelong learning. Nineteen-ninety-six was the European Year of Lifelong Learning, and mid-year the DfEE (1996) published its policy framework for lifetime learning.

The theoretical orientation of the work derives from critical theory and draws in varying measure from insights gained through feminist scholarship, action research, theoretical perspectives in psychology, qualitative research, post-modernism, and biographical approaches to research. I have tried to map such influences within the text, especially in Chapter 6, and remain unapologetic for the emphasis on theoretical underpinnings in the attempt to construct a relevant and reflexive sociology of learning.

This book questions the way in which student learning has, in the past, been conceptualised. In particular I take issue with the assumption that characterisations of the learning–teaching process make sense outside of a consideration of the sets of educational assumptions about learners and teachers within which such debates are pursued. In other words, it is not meaningful to engage in educational debates without first establishing the epistemological basis upon which such debates are founded. The importance of this assertion cannot be under-estimated. It takes as axiomatic the trite statement that 'knowledge is power'. More specifically the argument is one drawn from critical theory which illuminates power relationships between individuals and groups, and argues that predictive knowledge generated in the positivist paradigm and constructed meaning generated in the interpretive paradigm are dialectically inter-related rather than mutually exclusive. Habermas (1984) terms the former of these 'technical knowledge' and the latter 'practical knowledge'.

Technical knowledge is of itself unable to resolve arguments about the nature of learning, since it operates at the normative level of thinking about problems. Normative argument cannot take into account the values underpinning one thesis or another, it is evidential and can only provide evidence to be weighed towards one conclusion or another. In determining educational argument it is necessary to move beyond the normative/technical axis into the domain of worth, value and judgement.

Practical knowledge is knowledge grounded in the everyday world. In research such knowledge is rooted in the interpretivist/ constructivist paradigm and it has contributed greatly to our knowledge and understanding of the learning and teaching experience through in-depth analysis of learning environments, particularly classroom-based studies. Where the tradition has been open to criticism however is in the alleged naivety with which such research is pursued. In particular, studies that give substantial weight to biographical data, and to the achievement of identity, have been open to the specific criticism of individualisation. There is a strong political dimension to these debates. The primacy of the market in political social and economic life is in part a reflection of the denial of sociology that has become the hallmark of the New Right. In a market, individuals exercise free choice, fashion their own identities, and society, according to Thatcherite principles, does not exist. The allegations are serious indeed, in that they strike at the very heart of the nature of social science itself, *viz.* the scientific basis of the subject, its relationship to traditional science, the nature of sociological knowledge, our capacity to understand a social world that is constructed by individuals and groups. Central to this debate is the relationship between shared constructed meanings and existing economic systems and power relations. The feminist critique has also alerted us to the gendered nature of social and economic relations.

At the level of the organisation it is necessary to recognise that the increasing complexity of educational institutions and structures requires a theory of organisations that is both imaginative and adaptive. Interdisciplinary perspectives appear to have a major contribution to make here in as far as they can capture the extraordinary richness and diversity of campus life whilst avoiding the theoretical straightjacket that ignores the impact of other loci and foci. Current work being done in the field of educational management and administration, strongly influenced (although this is not always explicitly acknowledged) by postmodernist theories, not only recognises such complexity but takes its name from it:

> Complexity theory is concerned with the behaviour of 'complex adaptive systems', which are found everywhere and include brains, cells, ant hills, political parties and universities. They all have certain characteristics in common: each exists with numerous other complex adaptive systems, each has many levels of organisation and these constantly change as it gains experience, each anticipates the future and each is marked by perpetual novelty. (Griffiths 1997, p.376, citing Waldrop 1992, p.13)

Complexity theory encompasses chaos theory, catastrophe theory and systems failure theory and as such can direct attention to the importance of small events, unintended consequences and combinations of events and effects. There are three important benefits of such an approach. It opens a new avenue for research on organisations that is more in tune with the postmodernist agendas of complexity and diversity. It leads to a re-examination of old theories and possible re-conceptualisation and re-evaluation of those as a consequence. And it leads to new interest in describing and explaining complex phenomena, as theory development leads to further refinement of our taken-for-granted assumptions about what counts as evidence in research. Finally it is consistent with a proper emphasis on consideration of informal as well as formal systems.

It is central to the thesis of this book that the key to understanding lifelong learning lies in a new approach to thinking about education. This new approach does not claim to be value free, on the contrary. My argument draws upon critical theory in order to tread a path between the determinism of positivist/Marxist understanding of economic and social praxis, and the relativism of interactionist/ constructivist interpretations of the social world. Critical theorists propose a third approach to knowledge, emancipatory, which gives due emphasis to the historical context 'in which knowledge must be revised to reflect new historical conditions where people are not served by understandings generated previously' (Bloland 1997, p.12). Emancipatory knowledge synthesises technical and practical approaches to the world and recognises that human action is located within an historical context; our actions are situated historically, socially, politically and culturally. The research project is one which must take account of its responsibility to understand the social world of shared human interactions and meanings whilst at the same time recognising the dominant capitalist economic system within which such interactions and meanings are pursued. Central to this analysis is the observation that the sociological meta-categories of class, gender and race are interactive, are experienced differently between different societies and within societies. Ambiguity, dissonance, uncentredness are all expressions of the postmodern and must alert us to the complex life webs that we weave. For the educational researcher such considerations are pivotal.

The dialectical relationship between technical and practical knowledge is echoed in the learning and teaching model developed by Paulo Freire, which questions bureaucratic teaching and learning procedures in favour of a critical student-centred practicum. Central to this model is the notion of teacher and student as of equal status as subjects: 'the students – no longer docile listeners – are now critical co-investigators in dialogue with the teacher' (Freire 1972, p.54). Freire contrasts this model with the prevalent banking model of education, where 'knowledge is a gift bestowed by those who consider themselves knowledgeable upon those whom they consider to know nothing' (1972, p.46). This approach, which has been conceptualised as a 'dialectical learning relationship' (Fryer 1994, p.19), is considered to be particularly appropriate in informing an analysis of educational structures and processes which takes adequate account of the characteristics and needs of adult learners as well as a pervasive and inter-related range of social and political factors.

The contribution of the method of discourse analysis, as applied within the methodology of critical theory, to an understanding of the centrality of power relations in constructing access to and ownership of knowledge is a powerful one. Discourse analysis alerts us to the importance of scrutinising the language (and thereby the underlying assumptions) with which debates are cast. The legitimate focus of such work includes jargon, technical language, professional descriptions, lay theories, political interpretation, exhortation, conceptualisation, rhetoric, sound bites, catchphrases hyperbole, and will be located in both formal and informal, institutional and personal settings. Highlighting so-called 'icon' words and phrases used by proponents of a particular view or perspective is an especially powerful technique to acquire a purchase on the theoretical assumptions, stated or unstated, of that position. It is by the manipulation of image, language, metaphor and analysis that those who argue within educational debates manoeuvre themselves into and out of position. Influences upon the choice and use of iconic language include television, radio, the press, unions, professional associations, funding and quality bodies, students and teachers individually and collectively, education managers and academics. The task of the academic is to problematise taken-for-granted assumptions which are held to be self-evident wherever and whenever these occur. This task is a difficult one because it is radical, and as a radical project will question political correctness in educational thinking to the same extent as New Right thinking that conceptualises education markets as a good. A radical critique is by definition invariably unfashionable, and may be as uncomfortable for the exponent as for those whose arguments are subject to it.

Deconstructing educational discourse is postmodernist and post-structuralist both in its formulation and its process. The different identity profiles of the students in this study are reported in Chapters 3 and 4. They are found to be fragmented, kaleidoscopic, differentiated, and to defy characterisation and categorisation into neat ideal types or dimensions. The student identity profile is read as multi-dimensional, inhabiting deep and surface worlds, frequently surprising and self-effacing. Such a characterisation sits squarely within a postmodern society that gives centre stage to states of disorder, indeterminacy and undecidability.

Yet there is a scholarly attempt to categorise, codify, draw implications and make conclusions from the data. The tensions thus created between the partiality and disparateness of data and the synthesis and cohesiveness of analysis present a conundrum. A feeling of this is in the analysis of the approaches to learning taken by the adults in the present study. They vary in the extent to which they feel that they can engage with classroom-based teaching, group discussion of projects, self-directed learning, open learning, library-based research, iteration with assignment tasks, and so on. One of the lessons to be drawn from this finding is that questions of the kind 'how do I learn' (rather than 'learning how to learn', e.g. Brookfield 1986, p.65) are first order questions for learners and their tutors. There is no place for what Claxton terms 'outmoded implicit theories of learning' (1996, p.55) which delimit and restrict what counts as learning and what doesn't. The danger of individual implicit theories is quite clear; they are 'the residual schemata, or unconscious belief systems, left behind in the mind by previous experiences of all kinds, and which are brought to bear on current events in order to attribute significance and meaning to them' (Claxton 1996, p.45–6).

Another way of looking at this question is posed by Barnett, who suggests that there is a useful distinction to be made between the 'internal' and 'external' student:

> On the one hand, we have the student grappling with the interior demands of understanding, of inner conceptual struggle, of formulating coherent thoughts and ideas, and of definite and bold expression. This is a virtually invisible student. Sometimes, we

catch such students as they show themselves in their hesitant responses and uneasy formulations or, indeed, their silences. On the other hand we have the external student, the student picking up the messages of the wider world and responding more or less to them. This is the student occasionally mentioned in policy documents, whether of the state or even of the university itself. This external student also has, we should note, an invisibility about it; or rather a fictive character. It is a hypothetical student, an assumed student, a two-dimensional student largely passive in the face of the external demands which press themselves forward, simply acquiring uncritically the prescribed transferable skills and providing the sought-for human capital for the economy. (Barnett 1996, p.75)

The relationship between these two conceptions of the student is in fact illuminated by an understanding of the implicit tensions between psychological and sociological concerns about learning. Both disciplines have informed the way in which we think about educational issues, however the tensions between individual and socio-economically situated action, constructivist and positivist accounts, bears witness to the difficulty of any attempted reconciliation or mediation between the two.

Barnett's suggested solution lies in the notion of 'displacement':

In the end the student leaves her life-world cognitively speaking and enters the new world of the intellectual framework. The leaving and entering are not without difficulties and, being new, may generate anxiety ... The leaving of one's life-world need not be permanent. Indeed, the educational value of the displacement being suggested here is likely to be enhanced if, having entered the new world, the old can be revisited with the perspective of the new. Of course, such a revisiting is not straightforward. In such a situation, one is inhabiting two discourses at once: the discourse of immediate experience of the life-world; and interpreting that life-world in a theoretical discourse. There is an awkwardness in inhabiting two worlds at once; but there is also a wisdom that comes with informed detachment. (Barnett 1996, p.80–1)

Just as this book questions some prevailing asumptions which have been very influential in how adult learners have been viewed by researchers and policy makers, it also takes issue with much that is taken for granted in contemporary debate within and about post-compulsory education. A discourse analysis of substantive topics in this area reveals that there are some dangerous assumptions being relied upon that are largely unstated and unquestioned. Included in their number are distinctions that are made between adult learners and students, pedagogy and andragogy, continuing education and degree study, lifelong learning and vocational education, full time and part time, degree and sub-degree. These categories are shown in Chapter 3 to be artificial and misleading, a convenient shorthand which has served only to promote exclusive educational policies and practices, and to narrow rather than inform educational thought and action.

This book is essentially a critique of the dominant ideology which has elevated particular notions and conceptions of learning to the status of *cause célèbre* in contemporary discourse. Currently educationalists and policy makers have hijacked the term 'lifelong learning' claiming to have located a radical noumenon but in practice seeking only to lay a bridge to their own conservative agenda. In recent years, lifelong learning initiatives have been enacted by the European Commission, the Organisation for Economic Cooperation and Development, UNESCO and the Naples Communiqué. New multi-national organisations have been formed to promote lifelong learning, such as the European Lifelong Learning Initiative (ELLI) and the World Initiative on Lifelong Learning (WILL).

The disingenuousness of the notion of lifelong learning as widely interpreted can be illustrated by reference to the ELLI definition, cited with approval by Longworth and Davies (1996):

> Lifelong Learning is the development of human potential through a continuously supportive process which stimulates and empowers individuals to acquire all the knowledge, values, skills and understanding they will require throughout their lifetimes and to apply them with confidence, creativity and enjoyment in all roles, circumstances, and environments. (1996, p.22)

Because of its inexactness this is a definition which can mean all things to all people. It is subversive of real educational contexts since whilst it speaks of individuals acquiring values, it fails to acknowledge the key role that teachers and significant others play in education. Lifelong learning has much to say about the educational process, yet the role of the teacher is frequently separated out from the central discussion, as though teaching was incidental to learning. Those who champion learning from experience and competence-based qualifications such as NVQs may well be comfortable with such a view, yet it ignores the pivotal role played by teachers everywhere in fostering educational discourses, nurturing learners, and enabling them to benefit from the new learning environment. My suspicion is that there is a growing movement in education which purports to privilege empowerment of the individual learner, alongside large-scale policy initiatives on the part of multi-national industries and governments, thereby clouding the real impact of government policies of the Right throughout Europe and elsewhere which are anti-educational in that they are in effect disempowering learners through resource starvation, market-driven policies and sycophantic campaigns which offer the illusion that action is being taken to promote learning. Without real teachers, given real resources to empower students, lifelong learning will remain a slogan, a catch-phrase, a substitute for real action. There is a need to acknowledge that the real challenge of lifelong learning lies in critical analysis at a conceptual level and practitioner action, especially in relation to initial teacher training, teacher development and the socio-political context of educational sites.

The antidote to stifling individualistic accounts of learning is a social theory of learning that gives due weight to social, economic and cultural influences. The nub of the argument is that lifelong learning is essentially a model that demands social and political change, and it is that which distinguishes the concept from adult education. Lifelong learning envisages the creation of planned opportunities for adults to engage and re-engage with both formal and informal learning opportunities. This may involve a reconceptualisation of pre-school and school education involving a substantial redistribution of state educational resources away from initial education and towards recurrent education (Organisation for Economic Cooperation and Development (OECD) 1973). The far-reaching implications of such a strong model of lifelong learning for the organisation and funding of education have been recognised for some time. In contrast with the weak model, which sees lifelong learning essentially as second-chance education for adult returners, the implications of the strong model 'reach back into the later years and practices of compulsory schooling even to questions about primary schooling itself' (Duke 1982, p.326). The strong model requires availability throughout the lifespan, maximisation of choice, vocational and non-vocational provision, prioritisation for those currently excluded from provision, focus on personal and social skills development, collaborative programme design, avoidance of bureaucratic fragmentation of knowledge into narrow specialisms, social relevance, avoidance of separation between learning and career choice, action on economic, social and psychological problems and flexibility in development of the model to avoid rigid over-specification (Houghton and Richardson 1974). These features of a radical lifelong learning are echoed in the eight principles of recurrent education or lifelong learning advocated in the seminal OECD Report of 1973, cited in Duke (1982, pp.326–7):

(a) the last years of compulsory education should provide a curriculum that gives to each pupil a real choice between further study and work;

(b) access to post-compulsory education should be guaranteed at any time after leaving compulsory schooling;

(c) distribution of facilities should be such as to make education available to all individuals, wherever and whenever they need it;

(d) work and other social experience should be regarded as a basic element in admission rules and curricular design;

(e) it should be possible and important to pursue any career in an intermittent way, meaning an alternation between study and work;

(f) curricular design and content and teaching methodology should be designed in cooperation with the different interest groups involved (students, teachers, administrators, etc) and adapted to the interests and motivation of different age and social groups;

(g) degrees and certificates should not be looked upon as an 'end result' of an educational career but rather as steps and guides towards a process of lifelong education and lifelong career and personality development; and

(h) on completion of compulsory school each individual should be given a legal right to periods of educational leave of absence without risking the loss of his job and social security. (OECD 1973)

The extent to which these formulations represent a radical political agenda for education can be gauged by the observation that in no European Community state have these principles been enacted. They remain an ideal, a blueprint for reform, a template for the democratisation of education.

CHAPTER THREE

Lifelong Learning What?

This chapter reviews the themes and issues that are the central concern of this book and which support the argument that lifelong learning is a problematic concept. Many policy makers, practitioners and academics with an interest in education have persistently made the assumption that a concern with education equates to a concern with formal education, and that within formal education what counts is the period of schooling which follows infancy and precedes adulthood. Underlying the equation of formal education with initial education is the idea that education is complete at the end of it. It has been called a front-end model of education (e.g. Boyle 1982), and this idea underlies many peoples' understanding of what education means (see e.g. Blackstone 1997a). Thus governments have shown an insatiable appetite for data on the outputs of the formal education system, a preoccupation which can be traced back at least to Callaghan's Ruskin College speech in 1976 and which has informed most educational debates subsequently.

Practitioners in education, including teachers, lecturers, managers, administrators and other support staff, whether in the public or private sector, are primarily employed within educational institutions, and look to the system of formal education for their future economic well-being. Such employees will not unnaturally look to the formal system for solutions to educational issues, particularly when participation is dependent upon such institution-dependent notions as application, enrolment and registration.

Academics, however, should know better. Researchers have been nervous to let go of notions of 'scholarship', 'academic' or 'pure research', 'specialisms', 'expertise' and the 'scientific method'. We perpetuate the myth that education is a practice, and in so labelling it we separate it from what is everyday and for everyday.

The concern with formal education is also reflected in the research tradition that has attempted to describe institutions of varying types as 'learning organisations' (see e.g. Argyris and Schon 1978; Garratt 1990; Pedler, Burgoyne and Boydell 1991). The literature has been particularly extended by studies of private sector companies which seek to explain marketing success by pointing to institutional strategies and frameworks that foster and sustain not only learning within the organisation but learning *by* the organisation. Although it is highly tempting for managers to believe that through their influence organisations can learn and renovate, on examination such claims seem to be little more than prescriptions for amending organisational structures in such a way that they facilitate individual reflection and action learning on the part of those who are employed in them. The force of concepts such as organisation culture, subcultures and micro-politics resides in their power to explain why certain values, myths and stories appear to be more effectively nourished within one set of system conditions rather than another. However the extent to which individuals within the organisation subscribe to, act out or internalise those values and so on remains, as Hargreaves (1991) has noted, a matter of individual variation. What such studies do point our attention to, however, is the idea that for an effective learning environment to be in place attention must be paid both to the efficacy of individual learning strategies, and to the system resources including teaching inputs and the academic structure as well as access to facilities, resources and learning support.

The failures of the formal education system to realise a learning society have been well documented by, among others, the de-schoolers and the philosophers of the Left whose ideas were enthusiastically taken up by those who occupied universities in the UK and took to the streets of Paris in the late 1960s. This failure can be explained by recognising that formal education systems are neither resourced nor are they capable of sustaining a vision beyond the purpose for which they were developed, that is, to fulfil the demands of the market economy. In the UK context, the way in which the UK government has dealt with the issue of lifelong learning provides a case study of a powerful notion adopted and instrumentalised by government and used to generate bland policy commitments with few resource implications.

The government issued its White Paper, *Lifetime Learning: A Policy Framework* (DfEE 1996) during the European Year of Lifelong Learning. In it, it placed its targets for education and training, which are predicated upon narrow competence-based NVQs and the outcome-based Investors in People, within a lifetime learning and learning society context, whilst at the same time attempting to ensure that expectations about the role that government would/could play remained low:

> *Lifetime learning* is not a Government programme, or the property of one institution. It is a shared goal relating to the attitudes and behaviour of many employers, individuals and organisations. Government has a part to play but governments alone cannot achieve the cultural changes involved in making a reality of lifetime learning. (DfEE 1996, p.4)

The letter to institutions which accompanied the report clearly reveals the instrumentalism of the government's approach. The three points highlighted from earlier consultations on lifetime learning were:

- a growing awareness of the importance of lifetime learning in maintaining competitiveness and employability;
- the effectiveness of government policies in working with partners to promote a culture of lifetime learning;
- the effort and commitment at all levels to deliver lifetime learning on the ground. (Paice 1996 in DfEE 1996)

What is notable is that the spin put on the results of the consultation is confirmatory of the principles of competitiveness, market orientation and existing government policies designed to impose a competence-based qualifications framework linked fundamentally to the needs of business and industry. The assumption built into this model is that lifelong learning is the socio-cultural endorsement of the radical New Right education ideology. What is so insidious about this is that lifetime learning is reduced from its status as an emancipatory enabling framework for learning to the status of a policy expedience. In the government's hands lifelong learning was simply a new peg on which old failing policies could be hung. As with all rhetoric, lifelong learning is open to contradictory interpretations:

> We may now accept that recurrent education should be reserved to mean a strategy for the education system as a whole, and for change which implies and to some degree depends upon changes in other parts of the social structure, particularly in economic and social welfare policy. Also that, as a strategy for lifelong learning, it is inherently radical and far-reaching, though with gradualistic and tactical qualities. This is no guarantee that it cannot also be used further to entrench privilege and élitism, more effectively securing the advantages of the well educated. (Duke 1982, p.323)

Widening educational opportunities is not and has never been an exclusive project and there will ever be inequality at the point of take up even where there is equality of opportunity. What then are the characteristics of lifelong learning which are being thus undermined?

The concept of lifelong learning is not new. The term was recognised by Dewey (1916, p.51). The OECD and the Centre for Educational Research and Innovation committed themselves to recurrent education in the late 1960s. Jarl Bengtsson (1979), in a paper in the *World Yearbook of Education* titled 'The work/leisure/ education life cycle' used the synonymous term 'recurrent education' arguing that it has the capacity to change the dominant life cycle pattern from education–work–retirement to one in which the three main phases of life would be intermingled. However the economic implications of such a commitment were soon realised by governments and the idea was quickly sidelined by budget-conscious politicians. The idea has seen a resurgence in the last few years. Lifelong learning was recently adopted by UNESCO, and 1996 was the 'European Year of Lifelong Learning'.

The *locus classicus* (but see R. H. Dave 1976) of the emancipatory notion of lifelong learning is to be found in the work of Edmund King, whose paper 'Education for a communications society' reveals the core of his thinking:

> When talking of earlier educational idioms it was clear that people mainly thought of schools and colleges and similarly institutonalized provision ... In truth we need *a new system* which would encompass the most useful of those institutions and services but take on much more educational strength than

anything we know by bringing them effectively into play with each other ... Therefore for the third educational idiom it seems best to think of a *provisional school*, with a *conditional curriculum* dependent on completion outside, and with prime emphasis on preparation for autonomous learning through *the experiential dimension of education.* (King 1977, pp.25–6, original italics)

King's vision of a communications society foreshadowed the new learning environment that has been made possible through technological development and globalisation:

It would now be technologically possible for us all to have a domestic videophone, linked by perpetually orbiting satellites to almost limitless information and comment. The network of communications is not yet materially established, but in principle the possibilities of constant contact with learning (and feedback, or re-learning) can and should be incorporated into a network of education. (1977, p.25)

In perceiving the power and possibilities of a global communications network, the only point that King got wrong is the trivial one that the images are presently carried by terrestrial cables rather than orbiting satellites. Multi-media communication via the Internet is now making possible all the advantages of a 'network of education'. However we have yet to understand the implications for the formal education system of the new educational idiom. To do so it is necessary to unravel education from schooling, learning from teaching, and experience from expertise.

One formal education system which has been held up as a model for individual access to lifelong learning opportunities is the American post-secondary system:

Possibly as an expression of earlier pioneer and settler values, post-secondary education is seen as the principal means of subsequent economic, social and personal progress. Investment in individual educational achievement is seen as essential to personal comfort as perhaps we regard investment in healthcare. Further, post-secondary and higher education learning opportunities are seen as resources from which the individual learner may choose an appropriate learning programme. Flexibility, mobility, diversity and choice in post-secondary education are the key organising features around which popular

consent is mobilised and democratic participation is maintained.
(Robertson 1993, p.73)

Robertson points to the self-interest of academics and institutions as a key obstacle in the way of a new culture of learning which supports and promotes access to education. The new learning environment is one where learners can identify their own personal learning needs without what is seen as the constraining influence of lecturers:

> This will involve students being able to exercise greater choice within learning programmes, moving between academic and vocational or work-based learning experiences, with resources perhaps following students within and between institutions as they exercise their choices. (1993, p.74)

Robertson maintains that an essential part of the new flexibility and mobility for students is the development of a national credit framework, within which 'students can "trade", enabling them to register learning achievements from diverse sites of learning and negotiate the accumulation of that achievement towards recognised awards' (1993, p.75).

The notion that a market in credits empowers the learner has become an orthodoxy in the formal education system. The bureaucratic advantages for institutions of a framework of qualifications, interchangeable and based on standard sized units and levels are apparent. However it is essential that the assumptions underlying credit systems are unpacked, in order that the implications of the idea can be fully assessed.

Credit systems imply much more than the restructuring of courses into standard-size units of a specified level. Implicit in credit systems is the notion that each unit of credit is free-standing and therefore interchangeable with any other. Any pre-specification of combinations of units must, by definition, restrict the flexibility of the system, constraining student choice and reining in mobility. Typically, credit-basd programmes do not place such limitations on users. Thus, the National Open College Network (NOCN) bank of modules is available to member institutions, who can use them as building blocks for centre-devised programmes or singly as part-time courses. There is rarely full specification of the learning resources, specialist staffing or learning and teaching methods required to support each unit. It is therefore the validation process that guarantees a coherent programme of student learning. Cumulative and synoptic assessment is a method for integrating unit-based programmes, but it is rarely used since it restricts interchangeability of units and therefore flexibility. To this extent it has been argued that the inherent structure of credit-based programmes militates against integration of the learning experience. It is a major criticism of unitised programmes that they have led to fragmentation of learning within a technicist model of educational provision.

The problem is that it is idealistic to suppose that in a market-driven system of formal education individual learning needs count for much against system demands such as self-maintenance, accountability to funding bodies for efficiency savings and the next round of externally imposed performance indicators. The formalisation of education privileges system demands rather than learner needs:

> With knowledge goods and services having become commodities, exchanged for a price, it is the commodities that move in this pedagogical relationship [from supplier to consumer]. The consumer, especially in a unitized modular programme, is not fundamentally transformed but, instead, rakes up the credits for each unit which are then banked. Commodification means inertness: personal transformation is precluded. The student no longer gives of herself but expects that the commodity will already be of high quality; its assimilation can then safely be banked. In this economy, credits are given for safe banking, not for daring reinvention on the part of the student. (Barnett 1997, p.173)

There is, however, a danger in drawing too heavily on what Wrong has termed the oversocialised conception of man in modern sociology (Wrong 1961). To draw students in credit frameworks as loosely or passively engaging with a system over which they have little or no control may be to over-state the extent to which they make sense of the reality of mass higher education and make their way through it. Trowler has made a similar point about the way in which academics have been, wrongly in his view, characterised within a '"passive academic" model' (Trowler 1997, p.303). He argues that academics adopt a number of strategies in the face of the credit framework including a number of coping strategies, policy reinterpretation and reconstruction, policy manipulation, and 'swimming', which is

Trowler's term for those who are taking advantage and thriving within the credit framework. Key influencing factors on the strategies adopted include 'Epistemology ... educational ideology, organisational, professional, gender and other cultural "traffic"' (Trowler 1997, p.312).

A large number of studies either overtly or implicitly present an over-socialised model of students or academics as passive non-actors within the credit framework. In reality it is over-simplistic to suppose that groups of people that have been given labels of convenience (academic, student) will respond within a system in ways consistent with each other or consistent with themselves over time. The important lesson of a postmodernist perspective is that individuals have multiple 'selfs', groups form and make alliances, dissolve and reform, systems exhibit different characteristics at different times and within them organisational arrangements will at the same time be inclusive and exclusive depending on the context, the actors and the point of view. There is no linear relationship between intentions and consequences, nor should we look for one.

Within the access movement, an example of the way in which system demands are prioritised is in the continuing use of course retention rates as a key indicator of course effectiveness. Simply put, there is no more reason to suppose that a student who enters an access to HE course is any more likely to enter HE at the end of the course than there is to assume that those who embark on business studies courses will become business women or men. That access to HE has become a movement should of itself alert us to the fact that access is far more than a route for adult returners into higher education. Access embodies a whole set of values about valuing adult learning, equal opportunities, openness and responsiveness in education systems, lifelong learning, and so on. There are few alternatives for adults who wish to gain the confidence and capacity to return to formal study than to join one of the access courses, or indeed a pre-access course. Beasley's study of access route discontinuation in HE makes this point very clearly:

> Why some choose to discontinue is difficult if not impossible to define in simple terms nor fit 'neatly' into a theory or set of theories.
>
> An obvious factor is that adult students often have other commitments and many bring with them a legacy from past

educational experiences that is often negative. their motivation frequently seems to be a way to redress those negatives, to construct a 'new self' at times of crisis. In turn the educational experience they enter into often seems to 'release' or precipitate fresh crises as they come to understand themselves and the world in a different way.

The reasons given by these students for intermitting and/or discontinuing are as varied as the students themselves: to categorise or pigeonhole them was impossible, and at times frustrating as I wrestled with the 'interwoveness' of not only each student's interview, but also the way in which they connected to the others in the study.

I started out with the idea that to discontinue was negative, but now see how the experience itself was valuable and how positive most students were about their decision, whatever it was. Many have already returned or are about to. For others, the door remains open to return, whilst the rest feel they have reassessed their priorities and will not be going back. For nearly all, their time in HE had enabled them to make choices about what is most important to them on their terms. For adult returners, surely this is a crucial criterion of success? (Beasley 1996, p.7)

In order that priority of focus is given to learners, it is necessary to make a paradigm shift, to move outside of the formal education system in order to make constructive use of it:

To extract the full 'meaning' for education today we must draw imaginatively on support so far unused (and undiscovered). By its very nature that new education must extend throughout the whole of any society, now learning and expressing itself by every means of communication – technological, socio-economic and personal. (King 1977, p.26)

The aim of the educator within the new learning environment will be to reinstate the individual into the social contract within which educational provision is assured.

A recent example of the way in which categorisation blunts clarity in educational writing is in Barnett and Griffin (1997). In Stephen McNair's chapter, 'Is there a crisis? Does it matter?', he juxtaposes lifelong learning with school-based learning and makes the assumption that since lifelong learning operates within the arena of personal adult experience and knowledge that it is a radical notion:

> Precisely because adult learners are members of society not 'apprentices' preparing for entry to it, they have a different status, they have the right to challenge what is offered in the light of their own experience in the world, and of their rights as citizens. (McNair 1997, p.35)

In fact what is presented is far from radical on two counts. First it is an exclusive and conservative notion of lifelong learning, one which excludes learning that takes place in the early and later years of childhood. Second, it equates lifelong learning with adult learning from experience which carries the disadvantage of directing attention primarily to a view of adult learning that suggests that its key feature is a critical stance. It is not. Critique and interrogation of the status quo are indeed key aspects of well-planned adult learning experiences but they do not just happen, and sometimes they cannot be planned and indeed sometimes they happen outside of planned activities that are intended to produce them. A view of adult learning that casts adults as continually or even primarily engaged in radical critique is unrealistic.

It is important to understand the extent to which the debate about lifelong learning is bounded by discourse parameters, that is the degree to which the issue 'reflects a function of professional (rather than political) ideologies' (Griffin 1982, p.109), or what more recently Avis has termed as 'teacherly concerns' (Avis 1997, p.11). For the educational practitioner, therefore, 'discussion about lifelong education can be seen, in part, as an attempt to enhance the status of education by presenting a policy which puts education at the centre of society' (Lawson 1982, p.99). Similarly, when governments engage in discussion about lifelong learning this may be read as a reflection of a desire to prioritise education policies over other areas of economic and social life. The importance of social and economic inequality, as well as the influence of gender, have been highlighted in one of the studies carried out within the ESRC research programme on the learning society (Gorard *et al.* 1997). When policy makers adopt the concept of lifelong learning without specifying what resources are to be added in order to bring about the socio-political change that is at the heart of the concept and which gives it meaning, their claims seem to amount to little more than empty rhetoric and patronising generality.

Although this issue of the nature of adult learning has been widely debated, there are many who still fail to grasp the essential point that adults are divided by a common label. This point is well illustrated by Brookfield (1986) who, in his discussion of andragogy, correctly identifies it as an icon term around which adult educators seek to define both a theory and a set of practices, without really separating or seemingly understanding the difference between them. Knowles' (1980) conceptualisation of andragogy exposes the assumptions on which the notion rests:

1. Adults both desire and enact a tendency toward self-directedness as they mature, though they may be dependent in certain situations.

2. Adults' experiences are a rich source for learning. Adults learn more effectively through experiential techniques of education such as discussion or problem-solving.

3. Adults are aware of specific learning needs generated by real life tasks or problems. Adult education programmes, therefore, should be organised around 'life-application' categories and sequenced according to learners' readiness to learn.

4. Adults are competency based learners in that they wish to apply newly acquired skills or knowledge to their immediate circumstances. Adults are therefore 'performance-centred' in their orientation to learning. (Knowles 1980, p.92)

As Brookfield points out, the first assumption, which is at the conceptual core of andragogy, is highly questionable in that for many adults the 'attainment of a certain chronological age is most emphatically *not* accompanied by the exhibition of self-directedness' (1986, p.93). Further the characteristic is not exclusive to adults as some children exhibit it. The second assumption is one that most would concede, however it does again beg the question as to how far the principle is exclusive to adults. The third and fourth assumptions seem to give priority to a somewhat technical and reductionist view of knowledge. On the whole adults seem to value theory and issue-based work which may not have an immediate practical life application as much as 'performance-centred' or 'life-application' knowledge. In sum, what the notion of andragogy presents us with is a series of prescriptions which, taken along with other prescriptions, might guide curriculum designers to plan certain activities over others. What andragogy does not do is provide a conceptual rationale for a theory of learning or teaching, since it misrepresents both.

A further example of how research on adult learning has misrepresented its nature through categorisation is to be found in Innis and Shaw's (1997) account of a project designed to discover how students spend their study-related time. As they rightly note at the outset:

> It is important to define clearly what is considered to be study related (ie the business of the university) and what is nobody's business but the student's. In the event we attempted to discover how and where students spent all their time on campus, but only how and where they spent their study-related time off-campus. As we shall see later, problems of definition were largely avoided by identifying precisely the range of specific activities (and places) in which we were interested, thus avoiding some issues of misinterpretation. (Innis and Shaw 1997, pp.85–6)

Far from avoiding misinterpretation there are two key flaws in the described approach. First, the notion that what is study related is 'the business of the university' only makes sense if there is considered to be a separation between study-related aspects of student activity and other aspects of personal life, family, friendships, interests that somehow have no relationship to learning, which seems a preposterous idea. Second, the decision of on what to focus the study is resolved by an assertion of the researchers' interests ('specific activities ... in which we were interested') rather than the learners', which denies the possibility that the researchers' prior assumptions and preconceptions may be misplaced, or the capacity for the research process to be reflexive.

The sampling procedures employed also demonstrate how categorisation limits the scope of research. The researchers decided to exclude part-time students from the project 'since it was felt that part-time students' learning experiences were likely to be so significantly distinct that they would constitute a discrete sample in their own right and would therefore require their own instrument to be particularly sensitive to their experiences and scheduling issues' (Innis and Shaw 1997, pp.86–87). This seems to overplay the extent to which the categorisation of students as full-time or part-time has any significance in terms of need to work, domestic responsibilities, patterns of attendance and the like. It is increasingly unhelpful to think in terms of the outmoded categories of full-time and part-time students. Those labels are an administrative and funding convenience but tell us nothing about the learning experience of students on courses. Worse, the labels conceal some key characteristics of the student learning experience such as the extent to which full-time students need to take on paid employment in order to fund their education. In a survey of Glasgow Caledonian University students (Smith and Taylor 1997) a Scottish Low Pay Unit study disclosed that more than 77 per cent worked part time with almost 20 per cent holding down two part-time jobs. The average working week was over 15 hours with 20 per cent working more than 20 hours and over 5 per cent working more than 30 hours.

Within higher education there is currently a great deal of debate about student learning. Much of the discussion is informed by a model of student learning that recognises a number of different approaches to learning. The most common dimension that is used to describe what appear to be fundamental and dichotomous student approaches to learning is that of so-called deep and surface approaches to learning:

> It is typically assumed that students display particular approaches to learning in response to the perceived context, content and demands of their learning tasks. On the one hand, students are considered to exhibit a deep approach (or a 'meaning orientation') in so far as they acknowledge the more abstract forms of learning that are demanded in higher education and are motivated by the relevance of the syllabus to their own personal needs and interests. On the other hand, they are thought to exhibit a surface approach (or a 'reproducing orientation') in so far as they encounter an overloaded curriculum and methods of assessment that stress the superficial properties of the material that is to be learned. (Richardson 1997, pp.168–9)

Richardson points out that there is some evidence drawn from the literature that points to the impact of subject areas on different learning approaches, with arts students more likely to take a deep approach than science students, and also that students' approaches to learning are influenced by institutional factors, with heavy workloads and prescriptive learning regimes associated with a reproducing orientation, and freer learning and good teaching associated with a meaning orientation. More significant, however, is the observation that 'there is evidence that individual students adopt different approaches to studying in different contexts in response to the perceived demands of the immediate learning situation' (1997, p.169). In other words, students may adopt a strategic approach to their learning as a response to the different demands of different learning contexts as they experience them.

An important and related aspect is the extent to which student learning is characterised as an individual or social event. A strong case for the former view has been made within the field of adult learning by those who foreground adult's self-directedness as a key principle of adult learners which is an important principle of the concept of andragogy (Knowles 1980). On the other hand, the emphasis on an individualistic psychology of learning, once popular, now seems to be more commonly challenged by approaches that give weight to the situated nature of cognition (and thus to social aspects of learning), for example in the work of Claxton (1996).

The present study has been strongly informed by work that has argued a close association between student approaches to learning and learning outcomes (e.g. Gibbs 1992) and between student conceptions of learning and approaches to learning (Ramsden 1992; McKenzie and Scott 1993; Trigwell and Prosser 1996), although the association may be indirect in as far as students are revealed by this study to adopt a strategic approach to learning, encouraged to do so where their academic work is concerned perhaps by the demands of the academic structure within which they are pursuing their goal of successfully acquiring graduate status.

Some very influential work on student learning in higher education has been carried out by Biggs (Biggs and Collis 1982) whose Structures of Learning Outcomes (SOLO) taxonomy has informed much work in this area. His work has identified five levels of student learning, which can be seen as representing a continuum from a surface to a deep approach to learning. Gibbs points out how these levels may be used in higher education in determining grading and degree classification:

> Level 1: Ignorance: the learner reveals no correct knowledge about the question.

Level 2: Unistructural: the answer contains one correct feature or item of information.

Level 3: Multi-structural: the answer is list-like, containing a number of unconnected items.

Level 4: Relational: the answer relates components together to make a case or logical whole.

Level 5: Extended abstract: level 4 with, in addition, a connection to a related area of knowledge beyond the explicit demand of the question.

These categories have an intuitive relation to degree categories. Level 3 answers gain a pass, or if the list is long enough, a lower second, level 4 answers gain upper seconds and level 5 answers gain firsts. (Gibbs 1992, pp.151–2)

The difficulty with this schema is that such categories may be interpreted as mutually exclusive, as if students exhibit one or the other, a surface or a deep approach. In reality the picture is more complex, as will be seen in Chapter 4. There are real difficulties about the kind of implicit theories of learning that have underpinned what I have identified as an over-formalised conception of student learning. The effect of such theories upon research and practice has been quite negative in that they encourage a deficit model of mature student learning:

> Discussions about the role of mature students in higher education tend to stress their alleged needs rather than the potential benefits that they can bring. In particular, it seems to be quite widely held that mature students tend to lack the basic skills needed for effective study in higher education, and perhaps as a consequence mature candidates are less likely to be accepted onto degree-level courses than younger students (see Woodley 1981). The notion that there is a particular set of skills that constitutes effective studying and hence guarantees better learning outcomes is in fact open to serious question ... (Richardson 1994, p.309)

It is crucial to recognise that learning takes place in different ways and in different places and is not straightforwardly determined by ability or intelligence:

> The idea that 'ability', or 'intelligence', is some kind of mental
> capacity which people possess in varying degrees, and which
> partly determines their level of success at cognitive tasks, is no
> longer tenable ... but rather reflects the specific, and largely tacit,
> knowledge base that people possess about the particular domain
> ... Psychologists are coming to the view that 'ability' is often
> highly situation specific, and is better seen as a learnable tool-kit
> of cognitive strategies and resources. (Claxton 1996, p.55)

As Richardson (1995) points out, where universities claim to value
deep approaches to learning, evidenced through the assessment
criteria and their application when marking students' work, mature
students' 'approaches to studying even when assessed shortly after
their admission are more desirable than those of younger students
[which] means that the quality of courses in higher education will
actually be enriched by the admission of mature students, since it will
provide school-leavers with an opportunity to learn by example from
the mature students' superior approaches to learning' (Richardson
1995, p.15). It is however important to be careful when making claims
about 'superior approaches to learning' since, as has been noted
earlier, no one approach is universally more effective, even when
judged against similar institutional learning aims and purposes.
There is though broad agreement amongst researchers and
practitioners that it is deep approaches that the university should
encourage, even if the systems in place actually reward surface
approaches.

One of the arguments most often laid against admitting mature
students to higher education without their having traditional formal
entry qualifications is that these students are deficient in study skills.
However, there is a growing body of evidence (e.g. Trueman and
Hartley 1996; Richardson 1997) that there is no one set of skills that
can be said to prepare students for higher education and further that
the range of skills required for academic success are not dissimilar
from those required for the effective organisation of daily life,
including domestic labour, which is an area in which many mature
students are highly experienced. Notwithstanding such evidence the
crucial point to make is that it is implausible to try to generalise about
mature students in relation to their prospects and success at
university: as a group defined solely by age on entry they are as
dissimilar in as many if not more ways and senses than they are

similar. As Richardson notes, 'An unmarried mature student aged 21 living in a hall of residence is probably closer to a traditional entry student than is one aged 30 years, married and living at home with young children' (Richardson 1997, p.180).

The issues introduced in this chapter have some far-reaching consequences for how we think about adult learners and lifelong learning. Perhaps the most important is that difference and diversity are defining characteristics of the students and their approaches to learning. In a postmodern world, agreement about what counts as knowledge is problematic, and settlements are partial and variously constituted by students and teachers. In this context, where patterns emerge it is the responsibility of the researcher both to highlight them and to look for difference, contradiction and untidiness. Particularly important is to assess how far the process of doing research imposes an order that is illusory, draws parallels that are unsustainable and neglects the positive and constitutive capacity of individual and group difference. These principles have informed the discussion of the data that is presented in the following two chapters and the issue is revisited with specific reference to the interview study in Chapter 6.

CHAPTER FOUR

'Before I Never Looked in the Back'

This chapter presents the student experience of learning as recounted by a group of adult students mostly in further education and following access to higher education courses. The interview data on which this chapter is based was collected during the academic years 1996–7 and 1997–8. The manner of its collection and analysis is an important issue which is fully dealt with in Chapter 6. The data is organised under three headings or themes. Theme one is the course and the college, and is presented in this chapter. Theme two, the student learning process, and theme three, motivational factors, are presented in Chapter 5, in which the themes are depicted as a model of lifelong learning.

Theme One: the course and the college

The students were asked specifically about the ways in which the course and the college supported their learning experience and, conversely, ways in which the college and the course could do more to support them. Their responses were wide-ranging and seem to lend credence to the view that, in different ways, college matters. Also grouped into this theme are questions answered about the lecturers and the students' preferred mode of teaching.

Students in this study were all attending or had recently attended either an access to higher education course, or a foundation year course. Access and foundation year students were mostly co-taught within combined modular access/foundation year programmes. The foundation year students were all registered as full-time and on completion of their course were scheduled to progress to the local university which validated the course. Some of the access students were registered as part time and some as full time. Most intended to progress to the local university also, but some had not committed at the point of the interview. Regardless of which course the student was on, or whether the mode of study was full time or part time, the typical pattern of attendance at college was three or four days which comprised morning and/or afternoon sessions which were scheduled to allow for children to be ferried to and from school. Again, regardless of type of course or mode of study, paid work and/or benefits are an essential element of many students' further and higher education career:

Respondent (R): I had to find my own tuition fees which were about £900 so I sold my car for that and obviously I needed money so I work for Safeway. If I'd have had a grant I wouldn't work for Safeway as much as I do. I should get a grant when I'm at university.

Interviewer (I): How many hours do you work at Safeway?

R: I work between 8 and 10 hours on a Saturday and about 8 hours on Sundays and the good thing about Sunday is that it is double pay so instead of £3.78 I get nearly £8 per hour.

This student was not claiming any benefits but most were. One had been forced to rely on his parents when benefit was withdrawn:

I: Has money been a problem so far?

R: Yes. I've had to come off job seekers allowance and I'm not getting anything at the moment. The only money I'm getting is from my parents.

Some students were experiencing periods of poverty as a consequence of their decision to re-enter formal education:

I: Has money been a problem?

R: Yes

I: Do you get a grant?

R: Not as such, I applied for funding from this college, I'm not entitled to a grant, I'm on benefits. I have to pay my own petrol, I have to buy my own paper etc. Money is always a problem.

I: So you don't work at all?

R: No.

I: Do you mind telling me roughly what you have to live on?

R: £70 per week, that has to pay my debts, my bills, everything. There have been times when I have had £2 to last me a week ...

I: Will money continue to be a problem when you go on to higher education?

R: Yes for the forseeable future. I want to go to university, I'm not sure how I'm going to do it. I might have to go part-time to keep my benefits because the grants will not be enough for me to live on. I'm in rented accommodation and at the moment that rent is paid for me; if I get a grant that won't be the case...

For some students, support from the family comes through as an extremely important factor in helping them to complete the course, often providing a financial safety net:

I: Do you get a grant?

R: No, but I'm OK, I have a very supportive family, my parents don't live too far away...

I: Are you working at the moment?

R: Yes, part time. I work at the checkout at Asda [grimaces].

I: [Laughs] And you don't like it much?

R: Well it's in the evenings, the job is OK, the people I work with are fine, I could be doing a lot worse I suppose but it's not me ... it pays my bills.

There is no sense in the students' responses that when they describe their straitened circumstances they are angry or resentful, nor do they offer the view that the deal they have is other than it needs to be. There is an over-riding sense of stoical inevitability that characterises their view of their financial situation – they neither wish to harp on about money nor to complain:

I: Has the course caused any problems in your life?

R: No. Only the problems with the grant assessment, that's been bothering me...

I: You will get a grant then?

R: I've got a grant but I've come across a hurdle and they will reduce my grant slightly.

I: How much do you get?

R: The basic £1700 and the student loan. The problem I've had is the dependants' allowance which they've allowed me but because we receive family credit ... I took that as one that they don't take into account but they do.

I: Do you work at the moment?

R: No

I: Do you claim benefits?

R: Yes, we do. My husband's income is very low [Family Credit] ...

I: Do you think money will be a problem when you go on to higher education?

R: No more than it is now.

One separated student had some capital to draw upon to support herself and her children, but she found it increasingly difficult to balance the books:

R: He does provide a certain amount for me but that is not always possible for him in his situation either ... I have used access [fund], I have used the loan. I haven't yet used my overdraft facility with the bank. I was going to but I was lucky enough to receive a couple of thousand pounds worth of shares from the Halifax merger ... I thought if I can't make it through the summer I can use some of those shares although I don't want to, I want to keep them at the moment. I have a very small two-up two-down place ... and it runs very economically ... I can just about run my home, barely feed the children. I have to have extra ... My mum has offered to help me if I'm in a situation that I can't cope with. Others get more than I do on unemployment benefit.

To all the students the facilities and resources of the college were a major factor, either facilitating or inhibiting their learning. Roughly equal weight is given to physical resources and staff support and invariably the two are seen to go together:

I: Is there anything about the college which you feel supports your learning?

R: The word processor is useful for assignments and the staff who are on hand in the library if you get into trouble, not having a word processor myself.

This student also felt that the student group was a source of learning support to him, but had a concern about the number of groups in which he was expected to work:

R: I'm doing different subjects so I see different tutors and students ... I think it would be better if we were in the same group all the time.

I: Why?

R: I think it enhances learning really and the feedback off one another, you tend to get into tutors or students, you have to start again ... I suppose it encourages a family type situation or atmosphere.

However, an alternative view was presented:

I: Are you always in the same group for this course or do you move around groups?

R: We move around doing a cross-section of different subjects.

I: Do you like doing it that way or do you feel you would like to be with the same group all the time?

R: No I like mixing with different people.

The evocation of a family by the former student gives an interesting metaphorical edge to debates about the merits of course and modular structures. Using a family metaphor for a course may evoke a sense of mutuality and inter-dependence, even parity, although clearly families are characterised by a hierarchical structure. The language of the latter student is suggestive of a more public, transient unit, where exchanges take place and people move on. This seems to be the scenario evoked by another student:

R: [Tutors] have given me time and they really have been very sympathetic ... they don't know my situation, they don't know how much time I put in ... They can't treat us all individually because there are so many of us.

This student did appreciate the facilities available to her to support her learning, although there are some concerns about the support staff:

R: There are good study areas, I think the facilities are very good and the library is very good ... they help where they can ... the computers are there for us ... sometimes the technicians are not as helpful as they could be ... I've not always been able to get the help I've needed.

Another considers that 'the computer facilities are very good ... the library is very good, there are always enough books ... there are quiet tables ... the tutors are always very approachable' whilst another agrees 'If you go for help there is somebody there'. Facilities and staff to help with them are linked by these students, and we might think of this as a learning support framework with a number of important elements. If one is missing or inadequate the framework is weakened and the learning support is less effective. This is not to say that the students expected a great deal in the way of learning support. Several recognised that the policy of the college was that 'it encourages self-learning ... do it on your own'. The excitement of some students at the opportunity they have discovered provides a heart-warming and poignant counterpoint to some of the expressions of disappointment found elsewhere:

R: The library's brilliant and the resource centre is incredible ... I've been on the Internet – amazing ... the staff, the resource staff, the college itself, there is an atmosphere here that is supportive. The support services, people helping with personal problems, support and encouragement, and also those prepared to help with IT problems. They've all seen the problems before but they don't treat you as an idiot.

In the interviews the students were asked which mode of working they preferred and found most productive. Many assumed before they arrived in college that they would be expected to be independent learners from the start:

I: Do you find the institution treats you as an adult?

R: Yes.

I: How do you think it treats you as an adult?

R: A lot of the work we have to do on our own ...

I: So you are expected to be independent?

R: That's right. I thought there would be a bit of holding hands to start with and then gradually as the course progresses you would become more of an independent learner. From the start we were told that a lot of it is going to be on our own so in that sense it is adult oriented ... There could have been more support at the beginning of the course. I think it would have been available if needed, perhaps I didn't ask for it, maybe I should have.

The idea that adults should be able to work independently leads this student to expect little in the way of tutor support for his studies. Nor does he appear to expect to contribute to group work – he views the group as a resource:

I: Which aspects of work do you enjoy the most?

R: I can't say that I enjoy assignments but in some ways they are quite challenging to do. I'm getting more used to the word processor so sometimes it can be quite fun but I think it's the group work for me. I enjoy that the most.

I: Is that because you are good at it do you think?

R: Maybe, I enjoy listening really, I'm not a great talker.

I: You like to get hold of other peoples' ideas?

R: Yes.

When doing assignments, he prefers to work alone, because 'well it's your own work you see and if you are with a friend or a group of people there are too many distractions'. However, having tried an Open University course, he 'didn't feel that that was helpful ... I think this kind of course is better because you have to attend classes and that gives you more discipline'. The access or foundation course is commonly seen by students as an appropriate preparation for higher education:

R: No way could I have gone straight into A level courses or university. I couldn't have done it. I wasn't equipped, I didn't have the necessary knowledge in terms of IT or structure because the structure of learning has changed totally. Study skills is something I had never come across, essay plans I'd never done in my life. I'd never gone off and learned by myself, everything is so totally different that I would not have coped. I would have given up. This is a way of re-learning while I'm learning the things I need to know.

This student appears to be grasping that the notion of learning to learn is the essence of preparing for higher education. What is emerging is a quite complex pattern of learner behaviours which underlie the positionality of the student within the institution. Some procedures are seen of value and benefit, some not. Which are and which are not seems to depend at least in part on the approaches to learning taken by the student. For many of these adult learners, however, studying alone is the norm, and represents their preferred mode of working. One reports: 'When we've been put into groups I've worked with others but mainly I work on my own'. However, like the previous respondent, she does see some benefit in group work as a resource:

> *R:* I never feel that I have read enough when I discuss work. I always feel that I haven't put enough in or I haven't taken from a lecture what another student may have done and I always feel that I'm missing out – why didn't I see that? Sometimes other students enlighten me to things I have overlooked ...

One student uses the library to gather books and information from CD-Roms, and makes use of notes and articles provided by lecturers:

> *I:* How do you usually do your work, do you do it alone or with a friend or in a group?

> *R:* Alone. I do it at home. I've got my own room with the desk set up. All the books are in front of me ... I prefer to work alone.

Another appears to gain benefit from class discussion and collaborative working:

> *I:* Which aspects of the work do you enjoy the most?

> *R:* I like the assignments, I like the discussions in class, the fact that we can talk about what we are thinking as we are working. I like the class work – it has a better feel to it than in school where you had to sit there and be quiet ... People will help each other, they will explain points to each other.

> *I:* How do you usually do your work, do you work alone or with friends?

> *R:* For the most part I work alone, but I have worked with other people from time to time and sometimes it's good because we can sort of brainstorm each other, sometimes we'll just discuss [the subject] when we're in a group and you will pick up ideas from that. For the most part I tend to do most of mine at home on my own.

One student found some aspects of the course, including group discussions, a real problem for her:

I: Which aspects of the work that you've done so far do you like most? Have you done group work, essays, presentations etc.?

R: No, presentations I haven't done yet and I'm dreading it ... I quite enjoy written work because I'm fairly confident of my abilities ... I don't panic about things like that.

I: What do you like least?

R: ... The thing that I find most difficult is joining in the group discussions ... I work quite well on my own generally.

However, in terms of individual learning support, she seems to gain much from others in the group:

I: How important are the other students in your group in terms of mutual support?

R: I think we are all being very supportive towards each other. Every time someone has a problem it's a matter of concern to people. Nobody seems to just ignore anyone.

There is a popular view that mature students bring qualities such as confidence, maturity and independence with them into college and that these attributes help them to develop quickly as learners, and enable them to play an active part in enhancing collaborative learning. These notions clearly do have a basis in reality, since it is the expressed view of many tutors that mature students are generally enjoyable to teach for these kinds of reasons. Students may also share this conception, as one put it, 'From the start we were told that a lot of it is going to be on our own so in that sense it is adult orientated.' The student is both reporting a lecturer view about the nature of the programme and the model of student learning that is associated with it, and his own assumption about how adults should, in his view, be expected to be independent learners. Notwithstanding this, the students in this study shared a sense of trepidation and anxiety which should insert a note of caution into the way in which we sometimes take their skills and capabilities for granted. The data is suggestive of a need to foster and nurture their undoubted capacities, and it seems clear that the effective college can do much in this regard. There are some clear indications of the kinds of arrangements that are thought to be helpful and conversely that are felt to be unhelpful. The area of support that is most helpful, and that can give most concern when it is not forthcoming, is that provided by the tutor in relation to work that is set for assessment. One student expresses her concern quite graphically:

> *R:* ... If there was somewhere that I could go and have that extra tuition (for essay writing) ... I've handed in work and had it competely ripped apart and I've gone away and thought 'I'm not coming back' ... I cannot have it ripped apart when before everything I have worked at it, I have sat there, I have lost sleep, I've let things fall apart around me ... and I've really tried hard and I've got a D minus and 'poor structure, poor mapping – the information is there but I don't like your style'.

The student describes what amounts to a bruising experience and there is a sense of acute disappointment and dismay at what is seen as negative unhelpful feedback. Another student is unsatisfied with the tutor feedback on assessment:

> *R:* I seem to find that with every essay I get the same remark and if I had – if I'd have been told 'don't do it that way, do it this way', you know, given a little guidance, I might have felt better about things.

Equally important is the input that the tutor provides on the format of work required:

> *I:* What type of work do you like the least?

> *R:* In Biology it's the practical assignments, I haven't got a scooby on where to start on writing up the notes and theory side of a practical. They haven't given us a background on how to write up these things. I think it is totally different to writing up an essay ...

Strong views are also held about the organisation and management of the college and the course. For one student a difficulty is what she terms bureaucracy:

> *I:* Is there anything about the college that you feel gets in the way of your learning?

> *R:* Yes, the bureaucracy at times ... I understand the need for bureaucracy but it seems to filter down so many levels before it hits us ... if the bigwigs make decisions they are based on facts and figures on paper not on people ... we are people not facts and figures ... it is sad because people are latching on to the fact that they can carry on with their education, it doesn't matter if you've been out of the system for a while ... There were a lot of things at the beginning of the

course that did not gel, there were people who could not get to IT because their lessons clashed and IT is vital because all our assignments are supposed to be done on computer. They cannot be done on the computer if you haven't got your IT card, and you can't get your IT card unless you can go to IT lessons ... So some of the things didn't work at the start ... Some people have to come in for only one lesson in a day which can be a bit of a pain if you've got to organise children ...

All students had a clear idea about what tutors can contribute:

I: What's the most important thing that tutors do to help you learn?

R: I get a lot from sitting back and listening to the experience that they put over to us ... they give us so much it's inspiring.

I: This is a kind of paradox, on the one hand the tutor is imparting information and the other hand you're working individually and discovering things, and they are almost at extremes those two models. What you've suggested is that they are both very important, the one because it's inspiring and the other because it involves you in the activity.

R: It is their job to encourage us to go out there and use the available resources so that we can achieve what we want to rather than just sit there and absorb the information that they are giving and almost regurgitate what they are saying. It's up to us to learn how to learn and use what's around us.

The enthusiasm of the tutor, their teaching style and their expertise were often mentioned as key indicators of the 'good teacher'.

R: They are all good tutors here, they know their stuff and they come across well ... I think being enthusiastic about your subject has a great influence on me.

Clearly the arrangements in place at the beginning of the course are important in setting boundaries and expectations. If some students have high expectations about what the tutor will provide this can lead to disappointment

R: I think initially I could have done with more help in the beginning. My confidence was perhaps a bit lower than it is now ... I felt more help could have been given on a one to one, especially where choosing HE or university courses went in October.

Other structural arrangements that caused concern were the lack of tutorials, and underlying this is a clear indication of the centrality of tutor support:

I: How important are tutorials compared to class and group sessions?

R: We don't have many of those as such. They are not integrated into the course. They should be because they would be beneficial. As it is, you have to catch hold of your tutor and pin him down to a time when you can go and talk to him ... They don't always have the time to spend talking to you that you would appreciate. As mature students I think we need more reassurance and encouragement than young students do because we are aware of the pitfalls, because we are aware of the commitment we're putting in, and of how important it is. We are also aware of how big the drop is if we fail.

The discourse of the abyss evoked by this student lends weight to the view that the tutor–student relationship is a central feature of the learning process for mature students. The metaphor that is evoked is that of the tutor as a mountain guide, guiding the student along the edge of a precipice. In this relationship there is a clear expectation on the part of the student that the tutor will not decamp but will be there, available to offer essential instructions and advice. This reading is also supported by the many positive comments made to the interviewer about how the relationship works. The following two comments by different students encapsulate both the trepidation of the student early on in the course and how the tutor provides appropriate reassurance:

R: In psychology the first assignment I did I was very nervous of. The tutor sat down with me and said, 'you have no reason to worry about this, you can do it'. He also said that he saw no reason why I shouldn't go on to university and why I shouldn't get a degree. To say that up front based on the work and my attitude at the beginning of the course was brilliant encouragement.

R: I've found that I've gained an awful lot of confidence ... in a way that it's been reassurance that there's no reason why I shouldn't be able to do the course and no reason why I shouldn't be able to succeed if I keep putting in what time I can.

Some students expressed what are often regarded as outmoded notions of good teaching, where the tutor's role is one of transmitter of knowledge and wisdom to ignorant receptors. As one says, it is the tutor's 'ideas and knowledge they have that's the most important thing'. This leads him to enjoy a more traditional method of teaching:

> R: I think lectures are good. You can read something yourself, we're all novices really, you can all have your point of view but I think it helps if you have somebody who knows what they're talking about.

The lecturer is someone who is in a position to unravel and reveal some of the hidden mysteries of knowledge and learning:

> R: Before when I read a book, you know, when you have those little numbers and you look in the back to see what it means and where it comes from – before I never looked in the back. These things they sound trivial but I wouldn't have noticed the link before whereas now I would.

An alternative view is presented by another student, who seems to regard the tutor–student relationship as a more equal two-way process:

> R: I like the way we learn in psychology where we start off talking about a subject and we're all chipping in before he's got half way through and it evolves, but we're part of it, we're not being talked at or lectured to. We're involved in it.

Another student attributes such teaching methods to the age of the access student compared with younger ones:

> R: It's blatantly obvious when they talk to us they talk 'to' us rather than talking down to the younger generation.

Another aspect of this is a common point that was made relating to the tutors' ability to empathise with their students' learning needs and problems:

> R: The attitude of all the tutors is very encouraging, they seem to know what people's problems might be and rather than wait for someone to say anything, come out in class and say, 'Well I know you're all going to be feeling whatever' and you think it's not just me, things like not having written essays for twenty-odd years. You go there expecting that people expect you to be able to do it and all the tutors are well aware that you are not feeling confident in your abilities to do something like that, and they really do encourage you to do what you feel ... they seem to know what your problems might be before you reach them. I think they are very used to dealing with people, mature students basically ... they've seen it before.

One of a tutors' most valued resources is time, and it is also the scarcest. This student appreciated the extra help he received from his tutors:

> *R:* They always offer to stay behind if you need any help, they help you along – they try and push you along.

For another the support from both tutors and student services staff was similarly conceived as both helpful and over and above what might be expected:

> *I:* Is there anything about the college which you feel supports your learning and studying?

> *R:* Yes, they are very helpful. The student counsellor is extremely helpful with all personal problems. I've just had some problems with my grant assessment and she has helped me with that. As regards the studying the personal tutors are very helpful, any problems at all they seem to go out of their way to help you.

What is interesting about the data presented in this chapter and in the one following, is its inconclusiveness. This is really where the postmodernist lens can help analysis since above all it alerts the reflexive researcher to the dangers of introducing modernist assumptions about the purposes and experience of education, wittingly or not. The voice of the students suggests that their student self in post-compulsory education is both fragile and resilient. A variety of important factors – like the level of support from the partner and the broader family, financial concerns to do with grants and the need for part-time working, feelings of inadequacy brought on by returning to an institutional learning environment when previous experiences of formal education have often been negative and associated with low self-esteem and personal failure – combine to create a complex web, a multi-faceted aspect to the adult's being as a student. What seems clear though is that these aspects are interlinked. The socio-economic circumstances that create a need to work part time, sometimes in more than one job, create a framework in which family and personal relations become stretched and strained. Significant others can do much to support and bring on the student, whether they are partners, members of the broader family, peers, tutors or learning support staff. So can they impede the process of becoming and remaining a student. Similarly socio-economic conditions bear down on institutional arrangements, and impact upon course timetabling, assessment, tutorials, workload and, critically, the mediation of the educational practitioners assigned to support the student and the course.

The funding arrangements for further and higher education have been instrumental in progressively reducing both the actual contact time between teachers and students and the shared expectation about what constitutes an acceptable staff:student ratio in each sector. If teacher support for students is an important element in sustaining adults who wish to return to formal education from a variety of different starting points, as it appears to be, then the government needs to look again at the structural support that is built into the system of funding post-compulsory education. Further and higher education can only work with the resources that are available, and the only option for the large majority of colleges and universities when faced with reduced funding is to reduce the teaching support available for students. It is when institutions attempt to make good the deficit that is created, by increasing the amount of student-directed learning that is unsupported by teaching staff, that open learning initiatives which could otherwise gain broad support are, in the eyes of many staff, undermined. Of course, there is always the defence that for teachers to argue for more teaching simply amounts to special pleading. That is why it is the task of research to highlight the nature of arrangements that both support and undermine learners and learning, modifications to which are within the remit of educational practitioners and managers, and at the same time to clarify the linkages between the specificity of the immediate learning environment and the broader context which we look to government to shape.

CHAPTER FIVE

'I'm a Me'

This chapter presents the data which led to the development of the second and third themes of student learning.

Theme Two: the student learning process

The second theme that emerged from the data comprised some linked aspects of the student learning process. There appeared to be some very clear indications that the students in the study differed widely in terms of their approach to learning, conceptions of themselves as learners and ideas about what skills are required to be successful in higher education. The linkages between these aspects present a complex mosaic that is evidence of a broad spectrum of student experience and operation. However there was broad agreement that the key skills required to succeed in higher education clustered around time management, self-discipline and organisation. The requirement of attendance is seen as helpful in this context:

I: How important is the course in opening up higher education to you – would you have been able to manage without it?

R: I did some OU work at one time and I didn't feel that was helpful ... I think this kind of course is better because you have to attend classes and that gives you more discipline. So in that sense it would be useful to HE.

I: What skills would you say were essential for higher education?

R: I think discipline to hang on in there, to keep going when the going gets tough.

I: Do you feel that you have these skills?

R: I'm developing them better now, yes.

I: What do you think your strengths are?

R: The strength to overcome the stress of meeting deadlines.

I: Your weaknesses?

R: Not doing enough at home, although I do do quite a bit, it's sticking to it and not getting distracted which can happen.

Another student elaborates on the benefits of self-organisation for learning:

I: What would you say were your weaknesses?

R: Timetabling … if I haven't got a strict timetable I tend to put things off.

I: Does the course help you in that respect?

R: Yes, I've learnt in study skills how to organise my time and how to break down a task so that it is not enormous. That's been a big thing because that's helped me in a lot of other things as well … Breaking down a task makes it seem less overwhelming.

The student data was searched for evidence of surface or deep approaches to learning, with the expectation that it might show a preponderance of one or the other, and that it might indicate that there would be a progression from surface to deep approaches over time. There was certainly evidence that some strategies that could be associated with a surface approach to learning were being adopted. For one student preparing for essay writing involved 'gathering material, lots of note taking and reading … rough jottings and then sifting through any good points that I can use … With deadlines coming so close together I just do enough to think that I will do enough to get through, enough to pass.' However later he describes how 'At first with essays I described things a lot rather than evaluated', which suggests that a developmental process is in train in relation to his approach to learning, or at least that he recognises that there is a difference between descriptive and evaluative modes of working. His descriptions of himself as a learner go to show how complex such issues are and serve as a warning against the uncritical application of crude bipolar categorisations:

I: Do you think of yourself as a learner?

R: Yes.

I: Do you see that as an important part of you?

R: Yes, I hope I'm not going to be a perpetual student, I think it is important I do see myself as a learner.

I: What kind of learner would you describe yourself as?

R: I wouldn't say I'm quick to learn but I'm willing to learn, willing to take in new ideas, I don't get stuck in any ideologies or things like that.

I: Would you see yourself as receptive then?

R: Yes, but not gullible.

I: Do you think of yourself as a mature student?

R: No, immature student.

The data is elusive if the attempt is to characterise the approach to learning or the learner's conception of himself. It has a teasing, self-effacing, grounded quality that should alert us to the reality that the college and the course are a part of, but not the whole part, of the learning experience. What the course has done for this student is to help him to see himself in student mode, broadly conceived:

R: I know where I'm going more than before the course. I can see myself as a student now, I've got a bit more sense of direction, identity, status perhaps.

For many mature students entering higher education achieving the work appears to build a tension between feelings of community and shared experience on the one hand and isolation and individual differences on the other:

I: At what stage are you now?

R: I'm going into my second year. I don't think anything will stop me, my grades have not been good although I haven't failed anything ... For me this is a great achievement. I mix with the A and B grade students and they can't understand why I don't get the grades ... but I don't. But I will, I'll keep working at it.

I: Why do you think it might be that you are not getting As and Bs?

R: I've always felt that I'm not tuned the way they are, I'm more artistic than academic and I do try very hard to apply myself and I do an awful lot of work. I'll sit in the library for three days and work on something ...

Another student also found the work hard and seems to feel that as a result he has little choice about what approach to take to learning:

I: Do you finish working on a task when you feel you have done enough to pass or do you try to do more?

R: I try to stick to doing ... I just want to pass the course, I don't want to get no distinctions, I just want to get the 40 per cent pass and that is the general attitude throughout the course because it is so difficult.

An alternative perspective is demonstrated in the following excerpt, which draws on notions of space and extending boundaries rather than the inward pressure of difficult and onerous course tasks:

R: Before I started this course I had worked on computers but it was a case of ... routine. I have come into college and I have learnt why the computer does what it does and how it can help me and how I can go in and out of bits without damaging it, that was the biggest thing, if I break this computer I'm in trouble ... I can take a bit from there and move it across to there and use it, whereas before ... I wouldn't ever dream of going outside the parameters I was in ...

Perhaps the difference in perspective can in part be explained by the way in which the learning experience with computers that is described by this student is building upon prior knowledge and experience, which suggests the importance of this approach for course designers and tutors.

For another student the general approach to working seems largely determined by a wish to compensate for the failure of ineffective strategies:

R: I try and do as much as I possibly can. I came out of school with two A levels at low grades because at that stage I did do just enough, I think now I'm determined to prove that I can do a bit more than that really.

This sense of determination to succeed against a background of previously ineffective learning may be a significant influence upon students' conceptions of themselves as learners. Equally important, however, is that some students do appear to think of themselves as lifelong learners in a retrospective as well as prospective sense:

I: Do you think of yourself as a learner?

R: I suppose I do. I'm always curious, I always want to know, I always enjoyed learning at school and that has stayed with me I think.

I: So it's quite an important part of you, the fact that you see yourself as someone who wants to learn and is trying to learn?

R: Yes.

I: What sort of learner would you describe yourself as?

R: I was tempted to say a plodder, which is what I was at school but ... a life learner I think. I want to use what I learn in my life to either improve my life, to improve aspects of my life, or to help me get a job that I enjoy ... I would like to think that I will be working [in ten years time] and I know that I will still be learning, now I've started I don't think I can stop, I don't think I want to stop.

For another student learning was something that happened both in and out of formal settings:

I: Do you think of yourself as a learner?

R: Yes I do actually, all the years since I've been at school I certainly haven't stagnated at all, I've been learning about new things all the time, not just in a formal learning environment.

For some learning is something that is both an alternative to working and an integral part of job satisfaction:

I: Do you regard yourself as a learner?

R: Yes, I think I prefer learning to working.

I: So you see that as quite an important part of you?

R: Yes, when I finally do get a job I want to carry on learning, I don't want a job where once I've learnt everything I need to know all I've got to do is just carry on and regurgitate the same old thing. I want to keep learning ... I would like to do something that keeps me active in a learning capacity otherwise I will just get bored.

Despite the difficulties faced in terms of funding, personal finances, family pressures, and other pressing commitments, learning is seen by students as important, and for many the course helps them to become more effective learners. Learning is something that may often have been done ineffectively in the past, and the course provides opportunities for some students to mitigate such prior negative experience.

Students appear to take both surface and deep approaches to learning, that is, the same students adopt both strategies. Lifelong learning is a notion that is understood to mean lifetime openness to learning new things, but not necessarily in formal educational settings. Support staff and tutors are helpful to the learning process but not essential, although poor tutors and poor course organisation are particular barriers to effective learning. Learning needs to be organised, and formal educational settings can help in terms of requiring attendance, which offers the opportunity for the student to structure their learning programme and to keep on task. Organisational arrangements in colleges and universities can help or hinder the learning process, dependent upon their capacity for responsiveness to students' learning needs.

Theme Three: reasons for joining and staying the course

The third theme of student learning touches upon individual motivations, perseverence and determination to achieve goals that have often been firmly set. A characteristic of the students' expressed reasons for joining and staying the course is that they show a complete lack of equivocation; all reveal a deep-seated commitment to becoming a student and achieving a higher education qualification. However, these students are all progressing along the further/higher education pathway, they are survivors in a system in which many do not complete, and there is no data on the level of commitment and factors affecting the withdrawal of those adults. Amongst those interviewed, dissatisfaction with work and income emerged as a significant reason for joining the course:

*I:*Why did you decide to study at college?

R: I felt I wanted a better career structure, more long term, I was drifting a bit and out of work and it was now or never really I suppose.

Another answers:

R: I was 16, I'd left home, was living in a room on £18 per week ... realised that this wasn't fine, so I decided to go back and pursue the secretarial side of things ... I wasn't happy doing that, so I decided that it might be a good idea to get a qualification ... had a family ... and again I looked and thought it's time to re-educate myself ...

trained myself up and did a management course so that I could run the shop ...

Self-esteem, self-confidence and a desire for improvement feature strongly in some of the exchanges:

I: Why did you decide to study at college?

R: I ended up with £3.50 jobs ... I thought 'I'm not going to get any better jobs than this' ... I did care assisting for a time. I enjoyed it for a bit but then it gets you down, you get stuck in a rut ... there are better jobs out there and I know I could do better ... I just want to better myself so I can look back and think I have done as much as I can ... I was coming up to my 23rd birthday and I was doing jobs that 16-year-olds could be doing and it was a sort of panic thing. I thought 'I've got to sort myself out'.

For another student, going to university involves a reconstruction of who she is and how she is seen by others:

R: I went to a grammar school where I was in the slow stream from the word go – until I left. I was always told that I was a plodder, slow, stupid, whatever ... my long-term partner reinforced that view – coming to college. Initially it was a way of stopping myself going crazy at home because I couldn't get out to work. I got to college and suddenly people were saying, 'you could go to university'. Within three weeks I was thinking this myself. I can go to university, I am going to university. There is a whole life opened up, and I'm going for it ... I've suddenly seen something I wanted to do years ago and was told I wasn't capable of ... I loved school, I was top of the class, but it was the bottom class. I was never allowed to forget that. I liked learning, I wanted to go to college when I left school but I was always told that I'd never do it.

For another student college also represents a way of escaping from a pre-destined path:

I: Why did you decide to come to college?

R: In the hope of getting out of a rut. It's for myself too. I know there's no guarantee of getting a job at the end of it all but it's just so that I have something ... just to get an education ... I think that when you're a mature student you think this is another stab at it, maybe it's my last chance so I think that's when you try a little harder ... Getting a job where I don't have to work weekends, the hope that I'll be able to stand on my own two feet and not having to worry about having to have a part-time job, and not having to work at piddling little jobs anymore hopefully ... I think if I gave up now I would always look back and say, 'I gave up' – it's like you've come this far and now you're going to give up. I can't do that to myself, now I've taken that plunge I've got to keep going on.

For another student the mixture of career ambitions with a recognition that as she gets older she may be facing a 'last chance' prove to be strong motives:

I: Why did you decide to study at college – have your reasons or goals changed since you started?

R: They haven't changed since I started, I'd chosen to do environmental science. This farm needs to be run ecologically and I just wanted to know more about it and I want to know that I'm doing it right, so that was why I chose the subject. I chose to go on the foundation year course rather than apply directly to university because I thought 22 years since being at school, I needed to know how to learn again, and also because the sort of jobs I've been doing over the last few years have been low paid, casual. Looking towards the future I can't see myself doing that for very long ... I thought it was time for a change. I'd just turned 40 and that had a bit of an effect.

Another reveals a dogged determination to stay the course:

R: I don't think anything will stop me, for me this is a great achievement ... I'm very motivational and I will apply myself and I will put the time in so it's got to come in the end ... I'm very determined, if I set my mind to something then I don't like to fail, I make it work ... The incentive is that I will educate myself, I will be able to help my daughter and son if nothing else comes out of it ... I don't want to let myself down, I don't want to let anybody down, I've come this far ... It has woken up part of me.

Increased self-knowledge is also an outcome for another student:

I: When the going gets tough what keeps you going?

R: The goals. I'm a lot happier in myself now, I know what I want, I want to get a career. I'm determined.

Once the decision has been taken to embark on a route to higher education, there appears to be a considerable pay off for the students in this study; the data also reveal some negative consequences, although these are less apparent. Some of the most powerful benefits had to do with the way in which the learning experience impacted upon the students' feelings of self-worth:

> R: I think I get more respect than I used to get. I had very low self-esteem and I didn't get much respect off people because of that ... I want to do something a lot more positive, I feel like I want to do something useful, once I get through university I want to put something back into the world or the country.

For another student the difference has been dramatic:

> R: I have become me instead of being somebody's wife or somebody's mother or just somebody on the governing board. I'm a me and I have found that I like the me that's here ... I've been allowed to be curious, instead of being told it's nothing to do with you I've been told to go and find out.

For her, the experience of returning to formal education and the prospect of success appears to offer the ultimate life challenge:

> R: I have a determination that most mature students have got – we came into it with our eyes open, looking for the pitfalls before they happen. We try to cope with things, we look for problems and solve them before we get there – as adults we're aware that things don't run smoothly, we need to be in control, we're committed, if you're not 100 per cent committed you don't stay on the course and a lot of the ones who have dropped out were not committed ... The goal, the determination to succeed – I'm not doing it for anyone else. If I fail this I fail myself and I want to prove to myself that I'm capable of doing it, capable of achieving it ... I want to prove to myself that I can do it. I don't want to end up just sitting staring at four walls, I want more in my life than what I see in some of the people around me where I live.

These two extracts reveal an articulation of a struggle between different selfs, a former self and a present/future self. The former self is unfulfilled and recognised in some of those who come into contact with the student during everyday interaction. The present/future self is emergent, in control, capable and has a potential to be successful and to be fulfilled:

> I: Has being at college changed the way you think about yourself and the world?

R: Yes, I've always spoken as I find, it's boosted my confidence to think that I'm making waves in my life, I'm making things happen, I've got a goal I want to reach. I've got rewards over the last twelve months for what I've been putting in, whereas in other parts of my life I've put it in and found it to be a complete waste of time. The learning process has rewarded me.

There is also a negative aspect to the learning process, one that is often tied in with personal and emotional difficulties:

R: I find I do get stressed when I am revising or researching something. I like to be isolated and I live with my parents at the moment and they occasionally pop in and say hello and then you realise how stressed you are getting because you can't draw yourself away from your work.

For another student the work 'has brought on stress which has aggravated my illness' whilst for another 'It has shaken me up somewhat but I have no regrets. I have done extremely well to hold things together.'
Another student is able to rationalise the impact that the course has had on her own life and that of her peers:

R: Everybody has personal pressures as well ... we have homes to run, a lot of us have families, a lot of us have relationships, either stable or broken or new relationshps or whatever, and we all have commitments to our time, we all do our own shopping and our own cooking, cleaning and washing and the rest of it, that all has to be fitted in. We all have to work out our own modes of transport and allocate our time accordingly ... The first day here I thought 'I'm never going to cope with this'. I really was frightened to death but within three weeks it had all turned round.

There are clear indications that the experience of coming to college, doing the course, and aiming for higher education bring about substantial life changes. Students routinely speak of their experience within a discourse of dramatic and multiple change. There is not a uniform picture of a mature student that emerges from the interview data. If there is a common thread it is that the experience brings new responsibilities and challenges which are life altering and that require a process of adaptation. Adults don't become students when they join a course, they add 'student' to their other persona – as the last student said, 'that all has to be fitted in'. The issue of how we should proceed in finding out about student learning is an interesting one. There is substantial anecdotal and empirical evidence that people mean different things by leaning, and that they discount certain types of activity as learning. This issue is hinted at in the report of the National Advisory Group on Continuing Education and Lifelong Learning (NAGCELL), which advises caution in adopting an over-mechanistic interpretation of data on learning:

> First, it is a mistake to equate either learning or achievement with qualifications alone. Each is a valuable measure, but there is much important learning which does not lead to a qualification. Secondly, perhaps partly because of the first confusion, many people do not recognise, or describe activities they engage in as 'learning', even though an educator might regard them as such. Thirdly, much learning, especially in work and in the community, is directly related to solving practical problems and what is 'learned' again may not be recognised, or credited as such. (NAGCELL 1997, p.16)

There is a body of evidence, including some from the present study, which points to the pivotal importance of lecturers in the process of student learning. It is suggested here that this evidence can be summarised as follows: good lecturers are not an essential part of student learning but they can play a major part in orientating, guiding and facilitating the learning process; poor lecturers are detrimental to student learning and can demotivate, frustrate and block the learning process. Of course this bald statement needs clarifying and explaining. The student stories that have been told within this interview study and elsewhere strongly point to the conclusion that the role of the good lecturer will remain as central as it has ever been in supporting learners in their desire for advancement and fulfilment. There is, however, a need to be clear what is meant by good teaching. When students refer to good teaching, they are referring not only, or even necessarily at all, to teaching performance in the classroom, but to a broader sense which includes how the teacher motivates the student, how assessed work is received and returned, how the teacher anticipates problems the student may have with the learning materials and process. These are indicators which can have a major impact in encouraging positive approaches to learning:

> Studies have identified a number of factors which are, in effect, the obverse of factors which foster a surface approach, such as

intrinsic interest in the subject and freedom in learning. Freedom may involve choice over content or method of learning, or scope for intellectual independence. A crucial additional factor is 'perceived good teaching'. What 'good teaching' consists of has been identified through many studies of teaching processes which are associated with a deep approach. Four key elements have been identified and none concern lecturer's classroom performance. (Gibbs 1992, p.155).

These key elements are clearly outlined in a paper by Biggs (1989), and can be summarised as follows:

1. Motivational context

A deep approach to learning is more likely when students' motivation is intrinsic and when the student experiences a need to know something ... The motivational context is established by the emotional climate of the learning. While a positive emotional and motivational climate may be a necessary condition for deep learning, anxiety and instrumentalism may be sufficient conditions for surface learning.

2. Learner activity

Students need to be active rather than passive. Deep learning is associated with doing. If the learner is actively involved, then more connections will be made both with past learning and between new concepts. Doing is not sufficient for learning however. Learning activity must be planned, reflected upon and processed, and related to abstract conceptions ...

3. Interaction with others

It is often easier to negotiate meaning and to manipulate ideas with others than alone ... Interaction can take many forms other than conventional tutorials and seminars, and autonomous student groups and peer tutoring can be very effective ...

4. A well-structured knowledge base

Without existing concepts, it is impossible to make sense of new concepts. It is vital that students' existing knowledge and experience are brought to bear in learning. The subject matter being learnt must also be well structured and integrated ... (Biggs 1989)

The interview data generated in the present study point to a view of student learning which supports the key ideas identified in the work of Biggs and developed by Gibbs. The exploration of the interview data in fact highlighted three cross-cutting themes which recur sufficiently to justify the claim that they appear to be central to the way in which these adults conceived of their learning and its personal, organisational and social context:

1. the course and the college, including the ways the course and or the college supports and could do more to support the student, teachers and teaching, attendance patterns and funding issues;

2. the student learning process, including how the student characterises her/himself as a learner, different approaches taken to learning, individual studying patterns and various notions about what skills are required to succeed in higher education;

3. motivational factors, including why the student returned to formal education, reasons for staying and perceived benefits and pitfalls associated with becoming a student.

As shown in Figure 5.1 these themes can be represented as a model, but rather than a static one, one that rotates, expands and contracts, and is in continually varying relationship between its three parts, between each part and the whole and between it and other external and internal worlds.

These factors are consistent with the four key elements of teaching processes that are associated with a deep approach to learning, referred to above. It is suggested here that what lecturers claim to 'know' about students falls mainly within the first theme of matters relating to the course and the college. Students are typically seen in relation to their role as members of a course, within lecture, seminar or tutorial contexts. An institutional picture emerges of the good and bad student, and these characteristics are derived from ways in which the student does or does not interact with the taken-for-granted institutional mechanisms: attending classes, handing in work, sitting examinations, and making module choices. In this capacity the student is engaging with the institution in a formalised way and the relation-

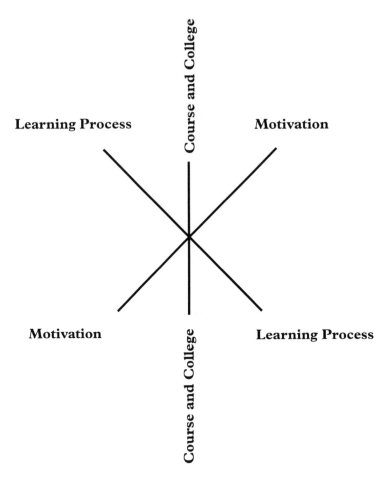

Figure 5.1 Cross-cutting themes in student learning

ship can be sustained and explained primarily at the level of mesa-analysis, where the analysis can be carried out within the discourse range of organisation theory, systems theory, or change management. The concomitant levels of analysis, micro-analysis and macro-analysis then refer, respectively, to the student's own private needs and wants, desires and fears – which I have clustered together as motivational factors in the model – and the broader context of education and social policies and their impact on becoming and remaining a student, including funding issues, demography and geography, social class, gender and ethnic differentiation.

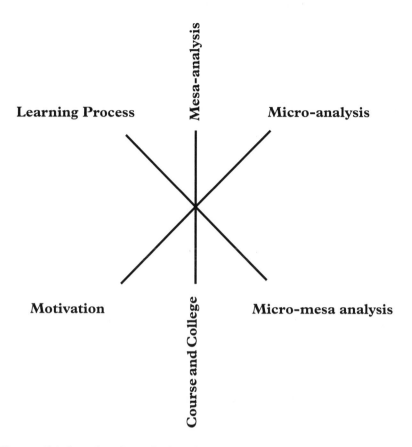

Figure 5.2 Levels of analysis of student learning

In terms of the model, the three cross-cutting themes operate at the micro (motivational), mesa (course and college) and micro-mesa (the student learning process) levels. Macro levels interconnect with all other levels. It is at the touching points, the interstices, where it might be possible to identify significant levers of student learning; equally it is at these touching points that substantial barriers in the way of student progress may also be located.

CHAPTER SIX

Darkness Visible, or Research in Post-Compulsory Education

Education should begin in research and end in research ... An education which does not begin by evoking initiative and end by encouraging it is wrong. For its whole aim is the production of active wisdom. (Whitehead 1932)

The study of further and higher education has in the past been characterised by a paucity of theoretical and methodological awareness. The same may to some extent be claimed also for the study of education as a whole, although school-based studies have generated some useful and interesting debates which have been informed by social theory. The Marxist studies of schooling by Willis (1977) and Corrigan (1979) in the UK and Bowles and Gintis (1976) in the USA particularly come to mind. I am aware however of no tradition of theoretically informed study of further education in particular. Four years ago, in an article for the *British Educational Research Journal* (Elliott 1994) I attempted an answer to the question 'why is research in further education largely under-valued by policy makers and practitioners alike?' The paper gave an historical context and argued that although there was a substantial amount of research being carried out on and in the sector, it had a low profile and seldom impacted on policy making or informed management decision making. Several years on I want to claim that the position is largely unchanged. Barriers to research in this area include: underfunding of staff development; inflexible staff contracts; high staff workloads; an absence of research contracts in FE; the active discouragement of 'academic drift' in FE colleges; prioritisation by managers of course development and teaching over research; limited access to library resources and the Internet; funding methodologies that do not reward research; continuing emphasis on short-term problem solving to meet college growth targets; a competitive FE culture that discourages collaborative research, e.g. networking; and an over-reliance on statistical and evaluative studies, many of which are instrumental and fail to address basic theoretical/political/philosophical/qualitative issues.

However, there are some positive and optimistic signs, some evidence of a growing interest in and demand for high quality work. Signs of increased activity include a growing number of postgraduate research degrees in post-compulsory education, an increasing use of consultancy and market research within the sector, development work and reflective practice by course teams; the setting up by the Further Education Development Agency (FEDA) of the Further Education Research Network, the launch at Lancaster in 1997 of a post-compulsory education symposium and special interest group within the British Educational Research Association, and the re-launch of the Further Education Research Association (FERA).

Nevertheless, it remains the case that the influence of modernist thinking on the study of this sector has been pervasive and research and policy agendas have been specified and delineated by the dominant stakeholders. This can be demonstrated by reference to the discourse through which the area of study is conducted and by the narrowness of its concerns and focus. Modernism is based upon the conviction that there are universal principles that underlie the state apparatus – of which education is a key part – and the cultural artefacts that it supports. These principles describe the boundaries within which ideologies – beliefs, attitudes and opinions – are expressed and exchanged. What is possible and what is not possible are clearly understood by all participants, who engage in a discourse that can be characterised as representing a community of values. Within modernism, reason and the scientific method are accorded high status and education is a means of promoting social justice, a transformative mechanism, a passport to economic well being, status and privilege. Higher education is seen as a route to high culture, middle-class values and social progress. Research is a means of advancing the frontiers of knowledge both to further understand the world and to improve it by reducing poverty, ill-health and instability.

Further education within the modernist project is the workshop that will provide the trained technicians and administrators to service and support the technological, scientific and bureaucratic needs of the modern economic order.

Postmodernism applies the concepts and terminology of poststructuralist analysis of language, made popular by writers such as Foucault (1979) and Derrida (1976), to social life. These ideas are centrally concerned with discontinuity, fragmentation, and disjuncture. The primacy of reason, order and science is replaced with deconstruction, difference and local knowledge. For the postmodernist it is the essential relationship between knowledge and power that forms the basis of the critique of modernism. Knowledge and power are manifested in the interactions between stakeholders, with struggles played out in a multiplicity of different contexts or sites. The discourses that take place within each site represent knowledge/power contestations, with the outcome inevitable: the dominance or hegemony of a prevailing discourse. The task of a postmodernist social science therefore is to characterise, through a study of discourses, knowledge/power contestations. In post- compulsory education this will involve focusing upon the plurality of identities in different sites and between sites including disciplines and departments (micro-analysis), institutions (mesa-analysis) and governments and quangos (macro-analysis).

There is, however, the unanswered question of where the postmodernist critique leads to. In its extreme form postmodernism leads to an absolute relativism. If there are no foundational values or principles then the most powerful forms and manifestations of knowledge will predominate. Postmodernism rejects meta-categories or meta-narratives such as equality, objectivity, social justice and social class, thus the arguments for widening access to higher education on the grounds of equity, for example, become a casualty of the perspective. Existing attempts to widen access are firmly grounded in a modernist paradigm, albeit one that has been broadened to take account of the mainstreaming of the idea of mass higher education. It appears impossible to reconcile the tensions between modernist and postmodernist perspectives. However, to understand and acknowledge that in the field of post-compulsory education, as in others, discourses can be read through modernist and postmodernist lenses should help to focus more accurately on what may and may not be possible for educators, academics, and policy makers. At the very least such a perspective should alert us to the danger of assuming that our own meta-narratives of access and equity may not be shared let alone actively promoted or legitimated by other stakeholders. Even less attractive may also be the postmodernist realisation that neither higher education institutions nor students may fit the romantic idealised conceptions that have characterised much previous work in this area.

There are two principles which can help researchers to escape from the straitjacket of formalisation, as I shall call the tendency to privilege the formal over the informal. The first is derived from Thomas Berger (1967): 'A way of seeing is also a way of not seeing'. In other words, researchers must attend to the certainty that preconceived assumptions or 'foreshadowed problems' (Malinowski 1922) will divert, confuse and mislead.

The second principle requires sociologists to become aware of the impact and implications of their own identity and social presence within the research site (Gouldner 1970; O'Neill 1972). To do this means not simply to recognise that the researcher's own values and dispositions should be declared and taken into account, but more significantly to appreciate the inherent conservatism of the research process. Whereas the whole point about being reflexive is that the status quo should be questioned and challenged, qualitative research methods, which have the potential to sensitise the researcher to the deep complexities of social life, have largely failed to escape from an empiricist paradigm (Schratz 1995). The inability of the academic study of education to come up with much beyond studies of the processes and products of schooling is an indictment of a research tradition which has allowed others to set its agenda. It is ironic that, even with the growth in interest in the notion of lifelong learning, the dominant paradigm of formalisation has ensured that the focus has been almost exclusively upon aspects of the participation of adults in the formal education systems of their countries, with very little within the research domain by way of a focus upon what Barnett (1994, p.179) has termed 'Life-World Becoming', which is characterised by reflective knowing, dialogue and argument as such and meta-learning. This open definition of learning situations is designed to turn attention away from systems of learning, that is the institutions with which we are familiar and which have been instrumental in our understanding of how learning takes place. It requires a substantial paradigm shift to acknowledge the learning that takes place outside of the formalised education structures of schools, colleges and universities which self-perpetuate by their very existence as major social institutions. Vast government resources are committed to them annually, education practitioners are employed within them and depend on their continuance for their livelihood, and the education system has inbuilt cross-phase linkages which are mutually supportive.

There is a parallel distinction that it is very important is made: that between continuing education and lifelong learning. The distinction is a critical one, since the two concepts have very different implications. Continuing education has its origins in the liberal-democratic tradition which has seen the establishment in the UK of an extraordinary range of adult education provision serving vocational, professional and general education needs. Lifelong learning, or recurrent education as it is alternatively known particularly in the European context, is a more radical concept which is predicated on a vision of an alternative education system, one which does not simply replicate existing inequalities in access to and take up of educational opportunities:

> The literature of recurrent and continuing education suggests that these ideas may stand for significantly different social policies for education, and that such differences are real despite the frequent ambiguity of the terms themselves. The social policy of continuing education has evolved from the liberal-democratic tradition of adult education itself, and it is concerned that the education system should serve the lifelong needs of people in all sectors of society, particularly those in relatively disadvantaged groups ... The social policy of recurrent education is much more of an alternative to the existing education system than a response to its inadequacies and failings: it is inclined to a political view of educational institutions, stressing the way in which they create and reinforce inequality ... (Griffin 1978, p.3)

The above distinction between the liberal-democratic and what we may term the radical concept of adult education has deep significance for the debate about the nature of the access to higher education movement. As Benn and Burton have noted:

> To attempt to understand Access to Higher Education provision
> as an educational social movement is to become caught up in a
> dialectical dilemma. Is Access allied to the older radical
> traditions of adult education through a collective emancipatory
> role or is its role to serve the educational needs of the individual
> student and/or the economic needs of society? (Benn and Burton
> 1995, p.444)

In their research Benn and Burton found that whilst access
practitioners espoused radical conceptions of access, they also held
views that supported a realist conservative conception of access as
serving individual/societal needs. They account for this by noting that
whilst an individual may hold to a radical conception of adult
education encompassing a commitment to social change through
targeting, 'these items may be forced into the background by more
urgent imperatives which stem from the Government's, and hence the
funding bodies', vision of education for social conformity and a
well-trained workforce [which] can lead to radical resistance,
non-rebellious resistance, inaction through indecision, or conformity
to hegemonic values' (Benn and Burton 1995, p.456).

   This study is an attempt to hold two aspects of the lifelong learning
debate together. These aspects are generally considered separately
and there is a substantial literature dealing with each, however they
are seldom inter-related. The two aspects are considerations about
students and their learning and considerations about the
socio-political context of learning. This project is an important one
since it can link micro- and macro-analysis and give a proper context
to mesa-analysis, at the level of the organisation. The point is well
brought out by Coare and Thomson in their study of adult learners:

> An historian recently commented that 'the present enthusiasm
> for life histories' among adult education researchers is in danger
> of 'obscuring the big picture and policy studies with fine,
> meaningless details' (Fieldhouse 1996: 119). Our response is
> that life stories about people's learning – such as the diaries used
> in this book – are not 'fine, meaningless details', but rather can
> illuminate the lived experience of the institutions, structures and
> relationships of education. Personal accounts evoke the myriad,
> complex motivations for participation in learning; they record
> the factors which make it difficult for people to participate in and
> benefit from education, and how these factors change

throughout people's lives; they reveal what forms and processes of education work, and sometimes don't work, for men and women: and they show what adults can get out of their learning, for themselves, their families and their communities. (Coare and Thomson 1996, p.201)

The interviews carried out within the present study were mostly conducted by a former foundation year student who had recently graduated with a good BA honours degree in Sociology and English, and who was in part-time work. She received the draft interview schedule and made a number of modifications to it which were agreed prior to the first interview taking place. The schedule was designed to be semi-structured, that is to guide the interview in the areas of interest. Some follow-up questions or probes were prepared in order to explore the respondent's underpinning concepts and views about their learning experience; these were needed for some of the interviews but not all – one of the noticeable differences between the transcripts is the degree to which some respondents flowed with the subject whilst others needed a good deal of coaxing in order to achieve a sense of their perspective on their higher education experience. As this was a foreshadowed problem with the conduct of the interviews, the issue was fully discussed between the interviewer and I at the outset. We discussed the use of interviews as conversations, the possible dangers of leading the respondent, and the benefits of the age, gender, life experience (including recently of further and higher education) of the interviewer. She and I were determined to try to reflect as accurately and in as much depth as possible the ups and downs of the students in the interview group, who were mostly preparing to access Level 1 of a modular undergraduate programme.

The interview data were transcribed in full with the students' contributions checked at least twice against the original voice recordings for accuracy. Each transcript was given a code in order that individual contributions could be identified without compromising the confidentiality of the subjects. Data category sheets were prepared which would allow for the collection and grouping of individual contributions around topics and themes that were identified as pertinent to the study. The identification of categories was based upon a number of sources, including previous work done in the field of student learning and the mature student experience in particular, information and experience drawn from several year's close engagement with an authorised validating agency for access to HE courses, and with a number of foundation year courses, the life experience of the main interviewer for the project, discussion on and subsequent design of the interview schedule itself and, of great importance, progressively focused analysis of the initial interviews, which informed the construction and achievement of the subsequent interviews.

The methodology of data analysis of the interviews followed closely the iterative model reported elsewhere (Elliott 1996, pp.47–49). The analysis of the qualitative interviews draws upon a five-stage procedure proposed by McCracken (1988) which incorporates the constant comparative method advocated by Glaser and Strauss (1967). This is an inductive form of data analysis in which the generation of theory is a continually developing process. Tentative categories are generated from the data, and subsequent data are used to 'test' the validity of those categories. This method is consistent both with the identification of foreshadowed problems, and the progressive focusing that is built into the research design. Each interview was carefully read through many times. An attempt was made to adhere to two important principles. The first principle was that during the first stage of analysis, individual statements were to be judged for 'intensive' meaning, that is, with little concern for their larger significance. An attempt was made to pay little attention to the supposed importance of the data to the research problem. The aim during the first stage of data analysis was to avoid unconsciously imposing preconceived understandings and assumptions upon the data (Rowan 1981). An important precondition, therefore, was that the researcher needed to be as aware as possible of the danger of in-built unexamined preconceptions and bias.

It was intended to delay, until the second stage of analysis, application of the ideas and concepts explored in the literature review to the interview data. During both the first and second stages, each interview was analysed as a unique project, and considered in isolation from the others. The experience of making a genuine attempt to adhere to these two principles was interesting. It is true to say that maintaining an open stance towards the data (Glaser and Strauss 1965), thus avoiding premature closure, whilst applying concepts generated from the review of the literature, appeared to pull in opposite directions. It would be fairer to say that a creative tension was maintained, where the focus would shift between the intrinsic meaning of the data and the extrinsic meanings and interpretations generated from the literature, personal experience and other influences. At best, an awareness of the problem of meaning imposition was achieved, and a genuine attempt to avoid it was made.

A significant amount of looping back did occur between the first and second stages, and between interviews, however, and McCracken's model of the stages of analysis of the long qualitative interview was adapted to take this into account (see Elliott 1996, p.48). The second stage of analysis thus involved developing the ideas which arose from the first stage, sorting and grouping those with a common focus, and expanding their implications. The more general interpretations generated were then related back to the whole transcript of the interview. As noted above, however, separating stage one and stage two is not always possible – nor, it can be argued, is it consistent with a developing and emergent analytical process.

In the third stage, analyses of each interview were compared, and further interpretations were developed of a more general nature. The fourth stage involved making judgements as to the emergent themes which were implicit in the interpretations of the interviews. A large number (13) of sub-themes were identified at this stage, but they were gradually subsumed within a smaller number (3), which can be termed 'meta-themes'. The final stage was a review and comparison of meta-themes across interviews, with the aim of generating analytic categories, and theory building. The three meta-themes in fact comprise the three section headings for the interview data analysis: the course and the college, the student learning process, and reasons for joining and staying the course.

There are a number of aspects concerning the context, focus, range and conclusions drawn from the study that point to the difficulty of researching this area of student learning. These are features that dog all research undertakings, but are seldom debated. However it seems important to raise them, not least because of the findings of the study that point to the multiple perspectives held by the students – as with the student, so with the researcher. If the task of postmodernist social science is to characterise knowledge/power contestations, as I would maintain it is, through a study of discourses, then it is necessary to apply this principle for proceeding to the research process itself. The research on which this book is based is reported as if it was a rationally conceived and implemented piece of academic work, that proceeded unproblematically from start to finish. That was not a conscious strategy, but arises as a result of the hegemony of the scientific method within academic discourse.

Michael Schratz (1995), in his excellent research primer for qualitative researchers, has alerted me to the extent to which even a research methodology that claims to be sensitised to the dangers of over-rationalisation seldom lives up to the grand claims that it makes. The dual tensions of 'bringing it off' – achieving the research project, meeting the deadline, keeping within budget, balancing research against other demands including teaching, administration, other institutional not to say personal and family responsibilities, and 'doing it right' – attributing ideas and concepts to their originators, critically examining taken-for-granted assumptions, interrogating the data, embracing reflexivity – both lead to feeling as if walking up a down escalator in rush hour. Add in the often unacknowledged fear and inward stress of admitting to oneself that the data is not consistent, that the analysis does not square up neatly, its partiality, that there are unexplained expressions of opinion, and that there hasn't been time to do a decent job, and it becomes less surprising that some colleagues decide after one project that a career in research is not for them. But who are we fooling if we let the illusion that research is a tidy and rational process hold sway, as it has done for so long? The discourse of respectability becomes a discourse of delusion for as long as researchers continue to adopt a supra-human position *vis-à-vis* their research undertakings and their subjects. If we know, as we do, that research in social science must take account of the multi-dimensional worlds of researcher and researched, and the overlapping crossing points between those worlds, then research that does not take full account of this cannot substantially advance our knowledge because it will be based upon an illusion.

This reading of research is consistent with an excellent analysis presented in the *Journal of Access Studies* by Shah (1994) who carried out a study of one mature student's experience of returning to education and her perceptions of identity and self-development in relation to this process. Drawing on the arguments of Foucault (1979) suggesting that we are implicated by and constructed within a multiplicity of complex and contradictory discourses or networks of power, she makes the crucial point that mature students 'do not constitute an homogenous group, they inhabit enormously diverse histories and populations' (Shah 1994, p.258). Her story of how she came to this view is important since it goes to illustrate the potential contribution of postmodernist analysis to education theories:

> Coming myself from a background which in terms of formal education was extremely limited, returning to education some 20 years or more later, and now working as a lecturer in further education and higher education, I have found myself constantly renegotiating my sense of self-identity. The recurring contradictions that I have experienced through this have made me realise that there is no singular or definitive 'real' me. Poststructuralist theory has given me a framework within which to articulate this process of ongoing change. (Shah 1994, p.259)

Shah traces her personal biography through a Muslim upbringing in Pakistan involving an informal education which prioritised domestic skills and gendered values, through a marriage which broke up following a move to Britain, the experience of being a single parent and subsequently enrolling at an adult education centre in a basic English class followed by 'Fresh Start for Women' and an access to cultural studies course. Her description of her experience of access is both funny and insightful in its recognition of the multiple realities inhabited by the learner:

> My identity as a student was ambiguous; I felt I wasn't a *real* student but an imitation. The image I held of real students – calm, collected, and completely submerged in study – did not fit my own experience. A closer approximation of this reality might have been 'manic mother in transit'. This scenario involved getting five young children up, fed, clothed and ready for school on time. Travelling to college via public transport to realise five minutes after the lesson had commenced that I had forgotten to give the youngest her packed lunch and the text I was supposed to have interrogated was still on the radiator drying. (Shah 1994, p.263)

Such studies are helpful in highlighting the dangers of adhering to over-prescriptive theories of learning. A primary consideration that applies to the present study is that it is to some degree self-serving, that is, as a study of the dimensions of student learning there is a foregrounding of meta-analysis and mesa-analysis, at the expense of micro-analysis. Several factors combine to bring this about: the present and previous jobs I have held in schools, colleges and universities lead to an automatic focus upon institutional issues; my present job privileges a focus upon FE/HE interaction; the interviewer has just completed her degree preceded by a foundation year course, perhaps reinforcing the formal context of educational organisations; the last year has seen an unusually large number of education policy initiatives impacting upon post-compulsory education, even for modern times (see Chapter 7), and coverage of these may have the effect of over-stating their effect and impact; whilst the interviewer has broadly similar characteristics to the respondents and has shown a high degree of empathy with their concerns, my interventions have necessarily refracted the shared discourses that she has accomplished; the interview data has a richness and depth that has really only been touched lightly and partially by the analysis so far. Time, competing tasks and the logistics of the publication process have combined to limit the analysis to what has been manageable rather than what could be possible. This may well have led to an under-estimation of the extent to which the respondents engage differently with the learning process, outside of the formal relationships and categories so far identified in the study; it has not been possible to reflect fully upon the range of policy initiatives still emerging at the time the book manuscript was submitted; confidentiality assurances and commitments mean that it has not been possible to draw the interview group together to offer them the opportunity to compare and contrast their experiences; nor has the opportunity been taken to check out the analysis with individual respondents. However, the analysis has been discussed with the interviewer who has contributed considerable insight and constructive comment; the research is being carried out at a time when the arrangements for the acceleration of the UK higher education system from an élite to a mass system are being stalled, principally through the changes in funding arrangements following the Dearing Report and the introduction of a means-tested standard tuition fee for all HE courses. The effects of this are being predicted but at the time of writing it is not known the extent of the impact on widening participation, the characteristics of those who do participate, and how the character of the learning process might shift within these external influences.

The difficulty of analysing contemporary events when policy is developing should not be under-estimated. The post-war settlement, which was characterised by broad agreement that a participative democratic project was an appropriate response to an imperialistic past, was fractured in the mid 1970s by Thatcherite market policies which vaunted individualism and self-interest. Arguably, with New Labour, the Blair project heralds the possibility of a new settlement, diluting rather than dismantling the market in education, and the replacement of shareholder politics, characterised by self-interest and the accumulation of personal wealth, by 'stakeholder' politics, characterised by citizenship and the accumulation of community resources. Presently there are indications and signals, buried within a mass of policy statements and initiatives, which point to a change of direction and a shift in emphasis, including some interesting examples of political alliances which cut across traditional party lines. However, the difficulty of 'situatedness' remains, for a study like this one that is concerned to 'read' social policy. The study is about issues and directions which are themselves part of a broader project which is still developing and shaping, and many of the unintended consequences of policy and policy contradictions are as yet still to be revealed or fully exposed. There is a particular difficulty in analysing the impact of access to higher education initiatives, since access spans both FE and HE and therefore stands at the interface between the two cultures which can complicate interpretation and policy analysis.

However, for all that, insofar as any piece of work is inevitably a snapshot, frozen at the point in time of its creation, this study cannot claim to be any more or less advantaged than others of its kind. What is highlighted by the issue of situatedness is the importance of taking studies in other contexts into account. Studies of lifelong learning that focus upon different points within the life span in a social policy context need fully to reflect upon the conditions of change and upon the learning issues that can be drawn from other work in the area. Practitioners and researchers have a responsibility to cooperate with each other in developing what Stenhouse (1979) called a 'contemporary history of education', that is, documented, accessible case studies of practitioner experience and development. Established organisations including the National Institute for Adult and Continuing Education, the new Further Education Research Network launched by the Further Education Development Agency, and the re-launched Further Education Research Association, all have a key role to play in supporting and fostering such development.

CHAPTER 7

Education, Education, Education Reports

In this chapter the key policy texts that were to appear during 1997 are summarised. It is difficult to think of another year in which so many reports and initiatives were produced. The significance of this output and the inter-relationships between them are considered in the following chapter.

The Kennedy Report

The Widening Participation Committee, chaired by Helena Kennedy, was set up by the Further Education Funding Council at the end of 1994 to advise it on achieving one of its key aims to promote access to FE for people who do not participate in education and training but who could benefit from doing so. Its report, *Learning Works: Widening Participation in Further Education* (FEFC 1997b) was widely acclaimed for addressing structural inequality in the further education system. The Campaign for Learning commented that '*Learning Works* places equity on a par with volume and quality in the learning society debate' (Campaign for Learning 1997, p.4). Its headline conclusions are:

1. The case for widening participation is irresistible.
   - Learning is central to economic prosperity and social cohesion
   - Equity dictates that all should have the opportunity to succeed

- A dramatic shift in policy is required to widen participation in post-16 learning and to create a self-perpetuating learning society.

2. The national strategy for widening participation must have further education at its core.

   - The unique contribution of further education at the heart of a self-perpetuating learning society must be recognised and celebrated
   - Only further education can deliver to all the entitlement to have an opportunity to achieve level 3
   - A consistent national policy framework must be created to develop the richness and diversity of further education.

3. Market principles alone will not widen participation.

   - Competetion in publicly-funded further education has resulted in improved responsiveness
   - Competition has also inhibited the collaboration needed to widen participation
   - Partnerships must be created to fill the strategic vacuum at the local level.

4. Funding is the most important lever for change.

   - Public investment in post-16 learning is substantial
   - A radical overhaul of the present arrangements is needed
   - Widening participation must be the key priority for public funding in post-16 learning.

5. The Council should develop its funding arrangements to widen participation.

   - Council funds influence the lives of millions of people
   - Changes in the distribution of funds are needed
   - Changes in the funding system must be planned to take into account the strategies needed to widen participation in the future.

6. New systems of financial support for students must be created.

   - Financial and practical support for learners is crucial for widening participation

- The present system is neither fair nor transparent; a root and branch review is needed
- Some changes must be made immediately.

7. We know how to widen participation – now we need to make it happen.

- There is good practice in widening participation, but it is not systematic, consistent or equitable
- The design and delivery of learning programmes must include extra help for people who have previously not succeeded
- Measuring participation and achievement must include the assessment of learning gain.

8. A coherent system of information, advice and guidance is essential to widen participation.

- Good quality information, advice and guidance are essential to widen participation
- Current provision is inadequate
- There should be an entitlement to information, advice and guidance about learning opportunities.

9. The demand for learning should be stimulated.

- There should be a national publicity campaign to stimulate the demand for learning
- Partnership approaches should stimulate demand locally
- The power of the media and of new technology must be harnessed to stimulate demand and make learning more accessible. (FEFC 1997b, pp.15–101)

The Kennedy Committee places the arguments which lie at the heart of its report firmly within the context of the need to bring about social cohesion, and the educational project is defined in human capital terms:

> Law, contract and economic rationality provide a necessary but insufficient basis for the stability and prosperity of post-industrial societies; these must also be leavened with reciprocity, moral obligation, duty towards community and trust. It is this 'social capital' which has a large and measurable economic value. A nation's well-being, as well as its ability to compete, is conditioned by a single pervasive cultural

characteristic – the level of social capital inherent in the society.
(1997b, p.16)

Within this project, education should play the key role as 'a source of
vitality ... the means by which the values and wisdom of a society are
shared and transmitted across the generations ... and creating
participating citizens' (pp.6–7). Against a background of 'the
enormous backlog caused by decades of under-achievement in which
national strategies for education and training have failed to make
significant inroads' (p.29) the report explicitly acknowledges that
current policy also has failed:

> To continue with current policy at a time of rapid change will
> widen the gulf between those who succeed in learning and those
> who do not, and puts at risk both social unity and economic
> prosperity. (p.15).

The extent to which the further education sector has been
under-valued, and its achievements in providing vocational training,
continuous learning, an alternative route to university, and a second
chance for under-achievers, is highlighted in the report, alongside the
negative consequences of the 'new ethos [which] has encouraged
colleges not just to be businesslike but to perform as if they were
businesses' (p.3). What has resulted is a haphazard pattern of
educational provision which lacks coherence:

> We are convinced that a national system of relatively auto-
> nomous providers, steered only by national arrangements,
> cannot adequately identify and achieve strategic goals at the local
> level ... The absence of a strategic dimension at local level, in our
> view, is a major weakness in the system which significantly
> reduces the potential for widening participation. (pp.38–9)

The proposals for revision of funding arrangements, which are
correctly identified as 'the most important lever for change' (p.43),
form a large part of the report's Agenda for Change:

- Launch government campaign 'Learning into the New
  Millenium: the Creation of a Learning Nation'

- Dedicate lottery funding to launch the 'Learning into the
  New Millenium' initiative

- Prioritise widening participation in the post-16 education
  agenda

- Redistribute public resources towards those with less success in earlier learning, moving towards equity of funding in post-16 education

- Establish a lifetime entitlement to education up to level 3, which is free for young people and those who are socially and economically deprived

- Create a national network of strategic partnerships to identify local need, stimulate demand, respond creatively and promote learning

- Encourage employers to provide learning centres linked to the 'University for Industry'; large firms would have to have their own, small firms would need to work together or with larger firms

- Reform the Council's funding mechanism to recognise levels of previous achievement and social and economic deprivation

- Create an expanded Council 'Access and Childcare Fund'

- Harness new technology for learning

- Launch a credit accumulation system, to be operative within five years

- Create new 'Pathways to Learning' – a unitised system for recognising achievement

- Take learning to the learner

- Reform financial support to students, including the benefit system in the interests of equity and promoting 'Welfare to Work through Learning'

- Launch a 'Charter for Learning'

- Create a 'Learning Regeneration Fund' at regional and subregional levels

- Establish a legal duty upon television to educate

- Set new national learning targets and local targets for participation. (pp.13–14)

The extent to which student financial support impacts upon participation and retention is underlined in the report, which acknowledges that 'The confusion and uncertainty which surround financial support for students create significant barriers to entering and staying in learning for those whose need is greatest' (p.72). The Committee is attracted to individual learning accounts in as far as they can provide an 'incentive to participate' (p.74); however there are some important caveats:

> Its potential must be investigated in depth. The introduction of any scheme, however, must be designed to take into account existing arrangements in further education. A scheme which relies heavily on contributions from employers will exclude those not in employment. Without positive support and guidance, those who are excluded – and therefore have little evidence of the benefits that accrue from learning – may have little or no incentive to use their accounts. (p.74)

The Dearing Report

The terms of reference of the National Committee of Inquiry into Higher Education's report *Higher Education in the Learning Society* (NCIHE 1997) made it clear that it was supposed to address some fundamental aspects of the way in which higher education is organised:

> To make recommendations on how the purposes, shape, structure, size and funding of higher education, including support for students, should develop to meet the needs of the United Kingdom over the next 20 years, recognising that higher education embraces teaching, learning, scholarship and research. (NCIHE 1997, p.3)

The vision of higher education presented in the introduction to the report makes it clear that it was to address directly the lifelong learning agenda:

> The purpose of education is life-enhancing: it contributes to the whole quality of life. This recognition of the purpose of higher education in the development of our people, our society, and our economy is central to our vision. In the next century, the economically successful nations will be those which become learning societies: where all are committed, through effective education and training, to lifelong learning. (1997, p.7)

This purpose is elaborated upon later in the report, where four main purposes of higher education are identified:

- to inspire and enable individuals to develop their capabilities to the highest potential levels throughout life, so that they grow intellectually, are well-equipped for work, can contribute effectively to society and achieve personal fulfilment;

- to increase knowledge and understanding for their own sake and to foster their application to the benefit of the economy and society;

- to serve the needs of an adaptable, sustainable, knowledge-based economy at local, regional and national levels;

- to play a major role in shaping a democratic, civilised, inclusive society. (p.72)

The vision for higher education is seen as one in which the UK develops over the next 20 years as a learning society, in which higher education makes a distinctive contribution. The report recognises that central to such a society will be 'a resumed expansion of student numbers, young and mature, full-time and part-time' (p.7), such that this aspect is given pride of place as the first of the 93 recommendations contained in the full report:

Recommendation 1 – We recommend to the Government that it should have a long term strategic aim of responding to increased demand for higher education, much of which we expect to be at sub-degree level; and that to this end, the cap on full-time undergraduate places should be lifted over the next two to three years and the cap on full-time sub-degree places should be lifted immediately. (p.100)

It is at this point that the report links, albeit not explicitly, to the Kennedy Report on widening participation in FE, and the Fryer Report on lifelong learning[1]. The report seeks to make the point that

---

1 Whilst the Fryer Report was not published until November 1997, some three months after Dearing, it is known that there was awareness within the Dearing Committee of the broad thrust, if not the detail, of Fryer's Report.

the objective of future recruitment should not simply be more students, but more different students:

> *Recommendation 2* – We recommend to the Government and the Funding Bodies that, when allocating funds for the expansion of higher education, they give priority to those institutions which can demonstrate a commitment to widening participation, and have in place a participation strategy, a mechanism for monitoring progress, and provision for review by the governing body of achievement. (p.107)

As well as diversity in the student body, the report also sees diversity in institutional character, mission and provision as a strength:

> We believe that the country must have higher education which, through excellence in its diverse purposes, can justifiably claim to be world class ... Institutions of higher education do not and will not fit into simple categories: they do and will emphasise different elements in their chosen purposes and activities: they are and will be diverse. (p.7–8)

In terms of the qualifications that are offered by the sector, however, the Committee was persuaded of the benefits of a framework which, although based on the existing system of diplomas and degrees[2], simplified the structure and made the inter-connectedness of qualifications more transparent:

> *Recommendation 22* – We recommend that the Government, the representative bodies, the Quality Assurance Agency, other awarding bodies and the organisations which oversee them, should endorse immediately the framework for higher education qualifications that we have proposed. (p.151)

The framework proposed a number of changes to existing programmes (see Figure 7.1) including:

- Higher National (HN) programmes to be structured so that the HNC is at level H1, and the HND at level H2, mirroring

2 It was widely thought within higher education that Dearing would propose a more radical restructuring of the qualifications available, perhaps moving to the two-year associate degree or higher national qualification as the norm, thereby reducing the time spent in higher education by most students following their first full-time qualification by a third from three years to two.

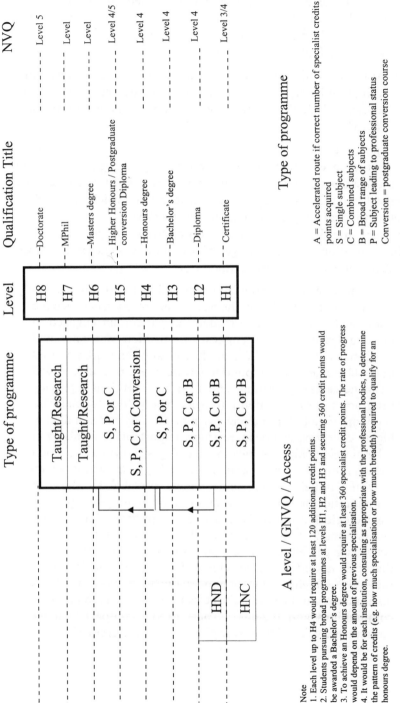

Type of programme	Level	Qualification Title		NVQ
	H8	Doctorate		Level 5
Taught/Research	H7	MPhil		Level
Taught/Research	H6	Masters degree		Level
S, P or C	H5	Higher Honours / Postgraduate conversion Diploma		Level 4/5
S, P, C or Conversion	H4	Honours degree		Level 4
S, P or C	H3	Bachelor's degree		Level 4
S, P, C or B	H2	Diploma		Level 4
S, P, C or B	H1	Certificate		Level 3/4
S, P, C or B				

HND

HNC

A level / GNVQ / Access

Type of programme

A = Accelerated route if correct number of specialist credits points acquired
S = Single subject
C = Combined subjects
B = Broad range of subjects
P = Subject leading to professional status
Conversion = postgraduate conversion course

Note
1. Each level up to H4 would require at least 120 additional credit points.
2. Students pursuing broad programmes at levels H1, H2 and H3 and securing 360 credit points would be awarded a Bachelor's degree.
3. To achieve an Honours degree would require at least 360 specialist credit points. The rate of progress would depend on the amount of previous specialisation.
4. It would be for each institution, consulting as appropriate with the professional bodies, to determine the pattern of credits (e.g. how much specialisation or how much breadth) required to qualify for an honours degree.

Figure 7.1 The Dearing qualifications framework for higher education

the Scottish practice of having a recognised qualification which represents the equivalent of one year's full-time work (the HNC) and one denoting the equivalent of two year's work (the HND).

- At level H4, the title 'Honours' to denote a level achieved in a single subject, a professional area or related subjects, which would include the existing combined honours programmes. (p.151)

The report identifies two key strategies to support lifelong learning. One is 'the development of distance learning through advances in communications and information technology', whilst conversely the other is 'the value of access to local institutions which are in close touch with local people and local needs' (p.195).

Present trends towards more home-based students accessing higher education through a range of local initiatives and partnerships are seen as a pattern for the future:

> There may well be, over the 20 year period we have been asked to consider, a material shift in the balance of provision between the traditional young full-time student, and the adult engaged in lifelong learning. This suggests to us that not only will institutions provide, as they have historically done, programmes in the liberal arts and respond to leisure interests, but there will be an increasing opportunity and need for institutions to provide programmes that respond to specifically local social and economic needs for lifelong learning ... The accessibility of higher education will be increasingly important. Franchising of programmes of higher education to colleges of further education (which is discussed in Chapters 10 and 16) is one way in which provision is being made more widely available for those in communities or from backgrounds for whom geographic or psychological distance is a barrier to participation ... Our analysis points to the greater benefits to be gained from a more active engagement by higher education institutions. We believe that regional and local engagement should be a clear element in the role of higher education over the next 20 years. Each institution should be clear about its mission in relation to local communities and regions as part of the compact that we advocate between higher education and society. (pp.195–7)

The findings of the report relating to the relationship between higher and further education are central to lifelong learning, and have generated some vigorous debate which reflects the high degree of engagement in this issue by all stakeholders concerned. The report appears to privilege the role that further education colleges can play in delivering higher education provision *at sub-degree level*:

> We are keen to see directly-funded sub-degree higher education develop as a special mission for further education colleges. In general, over time, we see much more of this level of provision being offered in these colleges, although we recognise that particular circumstances might apply in some cases. We also see no case for expanding degree or postgraduate level work in further education colleges. In our view, this extra discipline to the level of higher education qualifications offered by further and higher education institutions will offer each sector distinctive opportunities and best meet growing individual, local and national needs, although we recognise there may be different circumstances in the different countries of the UK. (p.260)

This leads directly to one of the key recommendations of the report:

> *Recommendation 67* – We recommend to the Government and the Funding Bodies that, in the medium term, priority in growth in sub-degree provision should be accorded to further education colleges; and that, wherever possible:

- more sub-degree provision should take place in further education colleges
- higher education provision in further education colleges should be funded directly
- there should be no growth in degree level qualifications offered by further education colleges. (p.260)

The report addresses what is seen as a tension between competition and collaboration between providers, such that 'there is a strong weight of feeling that competitive pressures have gone too far in promoting a climate which is antipathetic to collaboration, even where there would be strong educational or financial grounds in favour of individuals, departments or institutions working together' (p.261). There are two recommendations in the report which attempt to signal a remedy for this situation:

Recommendation 68 – We recommend to the Funding Bodies and the Research Councils that they review their mainstream teaching and research funding arrangements to ensure these do not discourage collaboration between institutions; and that, where appropriate, they encourage collaboration. We recommend to the Funding Bodies that they be prepared to use their funds on a revolving basis, bringing forward and offsetting annual allocations in support of collaboration which has a strong educational and financial rationale.

Recommendation 69 – We recommend to the Quality Assurance Agency that, as it develops its arrangements, it ensures that these arrangements do not discourage collaboration between institutions. (p.262)

Finally the report proposes that a quinquennial review of the state of the sector, followed by regular ten-yearly reviews, is needed:

Recommendation 88 – We recommend to the Government that, in five years' time and subsequently every ten years, it constitutes a UK-wide independent advisory committee with the task of assessing the state of higher education; advising the Government on its financing and on ways in which, in future years, it can best respond to national needs; on any action that may be needed to safeguard the character and autonomy of institutions; and, in particular, on any changes required in the level of student support and contributions from graduates in employment. (p.356)

The Fryer Report

The first report of the National Advisory Group for Continuing Education and Lifelong Learning, *Learning for the Twenty-First Century* (NAGCELL 1997), was commissioned by government to inform the proposed White Paper originally due in November 1997 but delayed until February 1998. The terms of reference of the advisory group were:

To advise the Secretary of State on matters concerning adult learning as required, and with particular reference to extending the inclusion in lifelong learning and work-based learning to those groups and individuals whose increased participation will contribute to improvements in employability, regeneration, capacity building, economic efficiency, social cohesion, independent living and citizenship generally; and to make proposals in respect of:

- The preparation of a Government White Paper on lifelong learning
- The strengthening of family and community learning
- The contribution of further and higher education to adult learning, having regard to relevant recommendations of the Kennedy Committee on widening participation in further education and the National Committee of Inquiry into the future of higher education
- Initiatives for development in the context of the University for Industry
- The development of learning towns and cities. (NAGCELL 1997, p.92)

Of the ten key agenda points that the report sets for the lifetime of the current parliament the first and key one is:

A new strategic framework is needed in place of the partial, fragmented, uneven and incomplete arrangements which exist in the United Kingdom. (p.4)

Those identified as casualties of the present arrangements in terms of their non-participation include unskilled manual workers, part-time and temporary workers, people without qualifications, unemployed people, some groups of women – notably lone parents, and those on the lowest incomes, those living in remote or isolated locations, some ethnic and linguistic minority groups, older adults, people with learning difficulties and/or disabilities, people with literacy and/or numeracy difficulties, ex-offenders, disaffected young adults and notably young men. The obstacles faced by these groups include shortage of the money for course fees and related expenses, lack of confidence, lack of outreach provision, lack of tutorial support when studying, lack of personal support, courses organised at inappropriate times and inaccessible places designed to be economic for the provider rather then the learner. This has all led to a situation, described in the report as 'not what we would find if we were already a genuinely learning society' (p.2), in which three-quarters of adults do not describe themselves as current learners, a third have not taken part in education or training since leaving school, more than 85 per cent of employees taking no part in job-related training, and most employers offering no training at all to employees (p.2).

The vision of the Report is that 'Learning must become normal and accessible, and learners must be put at the centre, taking increased ownership of their own learning and its management throughout life' (Fryer 1997a). Several core principles are identified:

- Coherence – The different stages, elements and levels of learning should all be compatible with each other and all be guided by the same core principles

- Equity – Lifelong learning should be for the many, not the few

- People before structures – The focus of policy and practice should be learners themselves and the quality and range of learning opportunities made available to them. This would shift attention away from structures and institutions, which should be regarded as more or less efficient mechanisms for the delivery of demonstrably high-quality learning in their given spheres

- Variety and diversity – Lifelong learning should be for all aspects of life and meet a variety of needs and objectives

- Lifelong learning should engage the whole of government – Whilst the Department for Education and Employment should properly be the main host and champion of lifelong learning, other departments of state should develop their own strategies and targets for the creation of a learning culture in this country and in its relationship with countries overseas

- Quality and flexibility – High quality and flexibility should be underpinned by inspection, audit, fostering a culture of self-assessment, and through improvements to the training, development and qualifications of teaching, advisory and learning support staff

- Effective partnerships – Local strategic partnerships, involving all with a legitimate voice and interest (including learners and potential learners themselves), should coordinate initiatives, pool resources, audit provision and establish agreed targets and plans for action

- Shared responsibility – Responsibility for lifelong learning and the development of a learning culture for all should be shared between Government, other public authorities and bodies, employers, providers and individuals

- Standards and benchmarks – These core principles should be subject to widespread consultation and further refinement and, once agreed, used as standards and benchmarks against which to measure present and future policy and practice at all levels from Government down. (pp.28–31)

In terms of the implementation of the lifelong learning agenda, the Fryer Report makes clear the special responsibility of education providers to ensure that their own contribution is clearly understood and focused, whilst ensuring inter-connectedness with other sectors and providers:

> All providers of learning will need to review their provision to ensure that it falls in line with the national strategy, vision for lifelong learning and core principles laid down to drive policy and practice. They should focus critically on how they should best meet the individual needs of learners identified in their own sphere of activity. Schools, colleges, universities, private trainers and those who provide or support learning in the workplace or community, will need to take stock of their own policies, practices and curricula. They will need to give particular attention to devising relevant approaches to outreach, guidance and staff development to support their contribution to making opportunities for lifelong learning available to all.

> Support for learners, in all of its many forms, will be vital to their success, but so too will be transparent links and pathways between different forms and levels of learning provision. One responsibility of those engaged in provision will be to examine and improve their relationships with other providers, in order to open these pathways, ridding them of any unnecessary encumbrances of complexity, lack of fit and bureaucracy. (p.72)

The reforms required to deliver the vision of a lifelong learning society are seen as comprising a major project:

> The scale of the task the Government has set can scarcely be exaggerated. For most people, and for many organisations (including some directly concerned with education), the case for

a major cultural shift still needs to be spelled out. We need a widespread understanding of the challenges the people of this country now face and genuine commitment to a new vision of lifelong learning to meet them. But we also need action, a start has to be made to deliver the vision in practice, at all levels and in ways which people notice and appreciate. To start the process, the White Paper should set out a radical programme of reforms, to carry the Government through at least one term of office, and beyond. (p.2)

These exhortations are, however, tempered with some realism with regard to the policy implications of developing a lifelong learning society:

We do not think that the only response should come from learning, nor do we claim that the development of a learning culture will itself produce automatic or ready made answers to the challenges our country now faces. To make such claims would be to foster illusions and would do damage to the promise of lifelong learning, when inevitably it failed to live up to them. Learning can make its valuable contribution to the resolution of problems, but it cannot and should not be a substitute for politics, economy and society. (p.11)

The report makes separate recommendations for further and higher Education. Further Education is seen to be at the heart of lifelong learning. 'Through further education adults of all ages, from sixteen upwards will be able to acquire new skills and competences, new knowledge and open up new horizons' (p.73). FE has the potential to link different aspects of peoples' lives: learning at work, social and economic regeneration, community development, leisure, sport and culture; support for basic skills development and advice and guidance services is given; staff efforts to widen participation should be supported and rewarded; representation from the colleges' local communities, including in governance, is seen as a way of ensuring effective community links, and there is support for strengthening colleges' research and intelligence skills, perhaps by closer working with local authorities, TECs and universities; a review of college missions, targets, partnerships and governance to ensure that they support a local culture of lifelong learning for all is recommended.

Higher education also has a vital role to play in the development of lifelong learning. 'The particular contribution of higher education lies in its proper concern with extending knowledge, and the skills of handling and applying knowledge in our society (p.74). This is to be achieved through excellence in teaching, research and dissemination, and a commitment to strengthening the quality of the professions and to continuing professional development; diversity of institutional character and provision is seen as beneficial; universities should develop with other providers and users, as centres of excellence in part-time study, distance learning and technology-based pro-grammes; accessibility is identified as a priority in relation to the whole range of activities and expertise provided; local, regional, national and international partnerships make a major contribution to lifelong learning and staff who develop these partnerships and disseminate the benefits of university learning should themselves be recognised and appropriately rewarded; students at all levels have a major contribution to make in assisting with audit and needs analysis, acting as mentors, participating in provision and as ambassadors and publicists for lifelong learning; governors and education managers should ensure that their missions, targets, partnerships, the curriculum offered, governance and forms of public accountability are kept under review to promote and monitor lifelong learning and widening participation.

The contribution of other providers such as the Workers' Ed-ucation Association, adult residential and specialist colleges and various independent foundations is also recognised: 'They too bring great expertise and long experience to the business of enhancing and sustaining the mosaic of learning provision in this country' (p.76). They are seen as a small, dedicated and valuable resource, and whilst their distinctive role is seen as important to overall lifelong learning provision, they are encouraged to work in partnership with other providers and stakeholders.

Although there is not room here to do justice to other key recommendations of the Fryer Report, there are important roles identified for libraries, guidance and advice services, staff training and development policies and quality assurance systems.

CHAPTER EIGHT

A Very Long
and Heavy Document

This final chapter will draw the threads of the thesis presented thus far together. It also offers a critique of some of the policy initiatives that have been introduced by successive governments, arguing that regardless of the political colour of their origin, education policies have failed to live up to the rhetoric of the policy texts and pronouncements that accompany them. Finally the chapter will offer an alternative vision for lifelong learning that privileges community over competition, actualisation over performance, achievement over certification, and participation over selection.

There is a modernist assumption built into much of the management of change literature that has been popularised by writers such as Peters (1989) and Peters and Waterman (1982), which is that change is positive and needs to be directed by management towards the goal of creating a community within the organisation. Corporate values and goals are seen as essential to the business re-engineering project. This emphasis draws quite strongly upon Eastern value systems:

> Eastern cultures view individual action and workplace processes within the context of community. This provides very different contexts for change. This includes paying greater attention to developing spirit among people as a foundation for the technical approach to change that we often take for granted in Western societies. In contrast with the Western obsession with performance and results, Eastern cultures pay equal if not greater attention (depending upon the specific culture) to the spirit of community. (Hallinger 1997, p.29)

If, however, the culture is one that is unsupportive of community values and instead promotes fragmentation and individualisation, even denies the existence of the concept of a society, then the spirit of the 'common wheel' may be elusive. The extent to which the New Right have eschewed one-nation Toryism in favour of market-based economic determinism, and to which New Labour have echoed these shifts, underline the difficulty. In policy terms it has become extremely difficult to argue convincingly without inhabiting the prevailing discourse of economic instrumentalism and performativity. In order to claim that lifelong learning should be supported by government it is necessary to point to the extent to which social and economic ends can be achieved, whilst arguments that are predicated upon more tenuous formulations of the learning society are likely to receive short shrift.

The report of the Kennedy Committee (FEFC 1997b) is a radical achievement that points to the shortcomings of the free market model for promoting lifelong learning. The agenda and action points advocated by the report explicitly and implicitly highlight that market principles will not achieve widening participation and that a coherent, planned and properly funded policy is essential to accelerate widening participation. The interim report, which appeared in the spring of 1997, gave an early indication of the thinking of the Committee in relation to the wasteful competition which had come to characterise the sector since the incorporation of FE colleges in 1993:

> The introduction of market principles to further education has allowed providers to move from dependence to independence and autonomy. Reforms have been successful in achieving growth in student numbers and some widening of participation. Along with improved responsiveness, however, there has also been wasteful competition as providers have competed for those students most likely to take part and succeed. (FEFC 1997c, p.4)

Notwithstanding its market discourse, in which terms like 'independence' and 'autonomy' are embedded within the report, it stands as a telling indictment of a government policy for further education that has failed learners and those who teach them. The lack of coherent national or local planning of FE provision has led to 'wasteful duplication' (FEFC 1997c, p.5), and large gaps in provision which cannot be resolved by the operations of a competitive education market, but only by 'Partnership approaches ... at the operational level to tackle those areas where, individually, partners have yet to make inroads' (FEFC 1997c: 5). This strategy is endorsed in the final report which leaves no room for doubt as to the legacy of failure left by the replacement of local authority led regional planning of further education provision by market-dominated approaches:

> ... in the rush away from planning and the heavy hand of the state, no clear strategic overview was developed, nor any statement of an overarching common purpose made. The way of avoiding destructive competition in the public sector is to bring people together around a clear and urgent common purpose. A process of continuous discussion creates alignments and collaborations as the sensible answer to the challenge .... public service values, which have been the pulse of further education, are finding little articulation in the new language of the market. (FEFC 1997b, 4–5)

There is a recognition in the report that knowledge and expertise in further education already exist for reaching and supporting under-represented groups. However, it finds that practice is variable, and that increasing access is not always followed up with strategies for success and progression. The report proposes wider dissemination of good practice, and higher recognition and status to be given to activities which widen participation. The report further recognises the efficiency gains which have been made within the sector since incorporation, but endorses the critique of those (e.g. Elliott and Crossley 1994) who have argued for some time that many FE colleges have lost sight of their *raison d'être* in their rush to become businesses and adopt business values. This has led colleges to adopt aggressive marketing strategies to pursue outcome-based funding which rewards colleges within a payment by results system which encourages 'too many colleges to go in pursuit of the students who are most likely to succeed' (FEFC 1997b, p.3). The consequence of such a policy has been growth in the overall number of students enrolled on FEFC-funded programmes, but little significant impact upon widening participation. Further, and this is a real concern, 'initiatives to include more working-class people, more disaffected young people, more women, more people from ethnic minority groups are being discontinued because they fall through the gaps in the system' (1997b, p.3).

The pivotal role of FE colleges in bringing about a lifelong learning society is fully acknowledged in the report. Their role is described as 'formidable': (FEFC 1997b, p.1), 'a vital engine not only of economic renewal but of social cohesion' (p.2). However, the report also correctly recognises that further education needs to be defined more broadly than simply that which is provided by FE colleges, to include provision by sixth forms, FE and sixth form colleges, LEA adult and community education, voluntary and community organisations, some HE provision, and education provided by employers, trade unions and independent training providers (FEFC 1997b, p.27). The report also notes that institutional provision is only a part of the picture, and that: 'with the revolutionary advances of technology, bricks and mortar are increasingly becoming less significant in the whole business of learning' (FEFC 1997b, p.8).

The Kennedy agenda was widely welcomed by FE providers for its determined expose of structural and funding inadequacies that had beset the sector since incorporation. In particular there were welcome signs that the previous invisibility of the sector, acknowledged in the report, would be addressed within the range of actions that were expected to follow the report. Such optimism was quickly blunted, however, by reports that Kennedy was persuaded at the eleventh hour to modify proposals in the early draft of the final report for a radical transfer of funding from the HE to the FE sector. It may well have been decided at that stage that a Labour government would in any case make a substantial proportion of the savings from the introduction of tuition fees to the HE sector available to fund the FE sector. As it is the report recommends equity in funding within the post-16 sector, and it is left unclear as to whether this includes HE or not; 'post-16 sector' is not specifically among the list of terms that are carefully defined in Chapter 2 of the report. There are signs of a fudge on this issue, since there are no specific proposals that relate to HE in the report, and the exact type of HE provision that is included in Kennedy's definition of further education is not specified. The inference throughout the report, however, and specifically in Chapter 4 on funding, is that the post-16 education that is being described is below levels H1 to H8 (see Figure 7.1) as defined within the report of the National Committee of Inquiry into Higher Education (NCIHE 1997, p.150), and it remains to be seen how far lifelong learning policy will take an integrative view of the whole of post-compulsory education and within that how many of its proposals impact directly upon higher education.

Helena Kennnedy, in her introduction to the Kennedy Report, refers to the trickle-down theory of education which assumes that to invest educational resources at the top end, i.e. with the ivory tower universities, is to ensure that the system as a whole will be ratcheted up. She presents the case for a redistribution of resources to further education, and in particular for the establishment of a 'Learning Regeneration Fund' which would draw together funding from national and European sources 'to pump-prime projects directed at widening participation in learning' (p.11). Other schemes which receive her support are the continuation of the ringfenced lottery funds, presently allocated to millenium projects, to create a 'Learning Nation Fund', creation of Funding Council incentives for widening participation initiatives, and reform of the benefits system which presently discourages participation: 'welfare to learning' as well as 'welfare to work'.

However imaginative and praiseworthy such schemes are, there are real questions about how far they can penetrate the inequalities that have led to the current position where access to further and higher educational opportunities is systematically and structurally closed off to those who are in poverty, in manual, unskilled, part-time or casual work and the unemployed. What is clear, however, is that in reaching a new consensus or settlement that lifelong learning is an issue that social and economic policies must address, there will be opportunities for specific initiatives to make a difference in terms of providing learning opportunities for particular disenfranchised groups. This provision will need to be adapted to local circumstances and provided flexibly, so that adults can take part alongside their existing commitments.

Formal educational institutions must be involved as they are where personnel and learning resources are intensively located, but universities, colleges and schools should not be relied upon for the totality of provision. Some learners will not be comfortable entering such buildings, and therefore it will be necessary to promote and provide access through community groups, associations, as well as in other public settings like libraries, shopping precincts, village halls and so on. There will also need to be some imaginatively designed learning programmes which can be accessed through open learning.

Book-, newspaper- and magazine-based materials will be required as well as IT-based information. Learning opportunities will need to be linked to peoples' interests so there will need to be accreditation opportunities for adult and continung education broadly conceived. Occupational, vocational, general and so-called recreational learning including sports and leisure activities must be interlinked through an imaginative and productive assessment and accreditation scheme, that can also acknowledge work and other forms of life experience. There are some initiatives that are under way or have already taken place which have been set up on the basis that a fresh imaginative approach is necessary. It is invidious to single one out for special attention or praise, but the campaign to raise the profile of adult learning and widen participation in adult education courses mounted by the organisation 'Northern Lights' exemplifies such a strategy:

Fun Campaign Brings Results

Victoria Tomlinson, Northern Lights

Lifelong learning may now be on many people's lips, but it's still a rather vague concept with very little meaning for the general public.

In 1995, North Yorkshire TEC approached Northern Lights, to ask us to make adults more aware of lifelong learning. We decided to focus on a tangible goal – to get more adults to sign up for courses – and to make the campaign relevant to the man and woman in the street. We were determined to take adult learning away from its sometimes 'worthy' image and give it the image of 'everybody's doing it'.

Time Barrier

We came up with a creative campaign which was a mix of practical tips for busy people - because research had shown that the biggest barrier to taking up learning was time, whether it was travel time (a big problem for people in a rural area) or making time to go on a course in a busy life – and we began to create startling headlines. Above all the campaign was lively and energetic. It had the title 'Just Do It' and everything about it shouted 'Let's take action'.

The key ingredients of this campaign were:

- carrying out a national Gallup survey which showed that more people say that learning something new makes them happier than sex or doing the lottery. 'Learning not sex' had wide national and local radio and press coverage; and although using sex can seem cheap, the TEC found that it generated discussion on all the right issues

- producing a lively advice leaflet, *Just Do It*, with ten people's practical tips on how they had made time to go back to learning in later life

- working with Hunter from the TV programme, the Gladiators, asking him to spend a morning learning new things and showing how easy it can be

- setting up and launching a series of courses in pubs, to help overcome the problems of travel in rural areas

- working out, with the help of colleges, the costs of typical courses and relating them to the cost of a burger or hiring a video, andpublicising the results

- highlighting that twice as many men as women go on courses and posing theories about why this should be and the effects on men

- running Bite Size Course Week, one hour courses on life's irritations, such as parking a car, choosing the right wine for a dinner party or cleaning a computer mouse. This was so successful that another week is being planned for 1998.

Ingredients for Success

There were several ingredients that made this campaign successful. The TEC used experts and listened to their advice. A steering group was set up from the TEC's amazing network of 250 or more training organisations – from libraries to colleges, community education to careers guidance. The steering group helped to make the creative ideas really workable and appealing. The support of the organisations meant that we could deliver activities such as Bite Size Week so successfully.

This campaign showed how working with an external organisation like Northern Lights can bring a fresh angle to difficult issues. In 1995, 52 per cent of adults in North Yorkshire planned to go on a course in the next two years. By 1997, this figure had risen to 67 per cent of adults planning to go on a course in the next year. A tangible success.

(http://www.lifelonglearning.co.uk/iln3000
/iln3003.htm Accessed 20.01.98)

It is original, innovative, and imaginative, whilst being clearly focused, targeted on a local area and engaged with popular concerns and interests. It is inclusive, and the scheme is notable for its deployment of the teaching resource outside educational institutions and within other settings in the community. It is initiatives of this kind, many of which are centred outside of traditional education providers, to which funding must be directed, working where appropriate in partnership with mainstream education providers. At the same time it is imperative that there is somewhere for those whose interests, skills and abilities are awakened to progress to. There is a place for formalised learning within the lifelong learning mosaic. Funding must support open access to it, as well as ensuring that those who make and take decisions are provided with sufficient incentives to make inter-connections between different levels of provision. Most important of all, government must not forget that whilst all have a role to play as stakeholders, elected representatives have the responsibility to foster the best equipped and best managed system that imagination and resources can provide. Policy has, therefore, a crucial role to play in leading development. Diversity is, as noted throughout this book, an essential characteristic of a lifelong learning society, and it is through an accumulation of diverse projects that such a society will come about. However, a lifelong learning society in which access to learning opportunities ceases to be an unexpected event cannot come about through the well-intentioned activities of those who believe that it is the right thing to do. There are more fundamental issues of equity and social justice, that only government has the resources and available strategies to address, that urgently need to be resolved.

It was an irony that in the same week that the interim report of the Kennedy Committee *Pathways to Success: The Widening Participation Committee Emerging Conclusions* (FEFC 1996b) was enthusiastically received throughout the post-compulsory sector, FE principals were stunned to receive two letters: one a letter from the FEFC announcing that the golden period of FE expansion was at an end; the other a letter received by the Council from Roger Dawe, Director General for Further and Higher Education and Youth Training at the DfEE, which contained this remarkable statement:

> The Council has a statutory duty to secure adequacy and sufficiency of further education provision across the country. The Government's commitment to cost-effective expansion of the further education sector has been set out in successive White Papers. Ministers recognise that the Council has already taken measures to improve its forecasting and control arrangements, and it is important that we continue jointly to make progress on these issues. But the unprecedented rate of expansion of student numbers, much of which is due to franchising, is far in excess of that envisaged by the Department or the Funding Council, and raises questions about how much is additional and about the maintenance of standards. It also raises questions about affordability, the appropriate balance of costs between taxpayers, employers and private individuals, and the potential impact upon other Departmental priorities.

> Ministers, therefore, now look to the Council to consider what steps are consistent with the containment of total expenditure in future years within the Government's planned levels of expenditure on FE, while allowing the sector to achieve reasonable and well-managed growth. (Dawe 1997, pp.1–2)

The spin put on this bombshell by the FEFC both highlights the contradictions within the government policy-in-action, and links the funding clawback, calculated to be £84 million or 2.7 per cent of the FEFC's annual grant, directly to the issue of widening participation:

> It means the Council having to find the £84 million out of its grant for 1997–8. This will reduce the funds available for all institutions next year. Including efficiency gains already in the pipeline, it will require colleges to make savings, on average, of around 8 per cent. The Council also expects the change in policy to slow down or even reverse growth in further education numbers, undermine college efforts to widen participation and create a major setback in progress towards the National Targets for Education and Training. (FEFC 1997c, p.1)

The FE colleges' representative body, the Association of Colleges (AoC), similarly drew attention to the contradictions revealed by this sudden turn of events:

> In the view of the AoC it is unacceptable that commitments to individual colleges through funding agreements for the current academic year should be unilaterally abrogated at a moment's notice.
>
> It is equally unacceptable that commitments to the sector as a whole to fund growth above FEFC targets at DLE rates, which has been part of the funding methodology since 1994/5 and of Government policy since 1992, should not now be honoured. (AoC 1997, p.1)

The decision was greeted in the educational press as 'a spectacular U-turn' (TES 1997, p.1), appearing to undermine terminally the vision contained in the government's *Lifetime Learning* document of new partnerships with 'the Government, employers, education and training providers, TECs, local authorities and individuals' (DfEE 1996, p.12).

The Dearing Committee's proposals for higher education were published in July 1997. There can be little doubt that the timing of the inquiry was convenient for the government. It was announced towards the end of its third consecutive term of office which effectively kept higher education off the political agenda for both main parties in the run up to the general election, ensuring that middle-class voters were not alienated on the sensitive issue of tuition fees. The findings of the report were widely leaked before its publication, particularly its recommendations on the charging of tuition fees to students. The New Labour government has long been persuaded by economic arguments that tuition fees were inevitable to avoid the onset of an HE funding crisis, but chose, in the face of the report's recommendations to the contrary, not to continue with the undergraduate maintenance award. David Blunkett, Secretary of State for Education and Employment, gave his governmental response to Dearing in a Commons statement on 23rd July 1997:

> We must develop a more efficient system than the present confusion of loans, grants and parental contributions. For lower-income families, instead of the remaining grant, students' living costs will be covered by a maintenance loan of the same

value as the current grant and loan package. An additional maintenance loan equivalent to the tuition fee will be available to students from higher-income families. We shall, however, ensure that the poorest students do not have to pay fees. That is the best way of encouraging access to free education for the least well-off. We are equally determined to ensure that there is no increase in parental contributions.

(http://www.parliament.the-stationery-office.co.uk/pa/cm1997 98/cmhansard/cm970723/debtext/70723-22.htm#70723-22_s pmin2 Accessed 24.07.97)

The announcement of a means tested tuition fee up to a per capita maximum of £1000 per year – made within a few hours of publication of the Dearing Report – took most observers by surprise and not unnaturally the tuition fee issue became the focus of most comment and some student demonstrations in the months following.[1] The government's radical tuition fee policy flew in the face of Dearing's funding proposals which were predicated on a concern that abolishing the maintenance grant would be tantamount to ensuring that socially and economically disadvantaged students were excluded from higher education in the learning society: 'I would say that the government system will leave those from poorer backgrounds with bigger debts' (Dearing 1997: 3). Baroness Blackstone, the further and higher education minister, appeared to confirm this in admitting that government funding proposals would mean wealthy students 'still paying less in terms of the loan repayments than a student from a low-income family who will have a somewhat higher loan' (Blackstone 1997, p.1). This appears at odds with the pivotal equality of access principle within Dearing, that 'individuals are not denied access to higher education through lack of financial means' (NCIHE 1997, p.85). Reportedly, 'The committee had favoured tuition fees rather than changes to maintenance arrangements because it wanted to ensure the extra money went into the sector' (Swain 1997, p.3). However it soon became apparent that despite reassurances to the

---

1 Although the NUS was widely reported as having been brought 'on side' by late government modifications to Dearing's preferred funding option – see, for example the *THES* front page lead story by Tony Tysome, 'Students stitch up Ron' (*THES* 1997b, p.1).

contrary [2] such faith was entirely misplaced when the government made clear towards the end of 1997 that not all of the funding raised by tuition fees would remain within the higher education sector. This was a further reminder that government was to be more influenced by the Kennedy agenda for widening participation in further education than by Dearing's proposals for higher education. The National Advisory Group on the lifelong learning White Paper left no doubt as to where government priorities in relation to lifelong learning were:

> We couldn't carry on with the current situation – full-time students, all in big institutions, studying for three years. There is a totally different conception of how it will work in the future. It is a radical shift and it will not work on the old models. (Fryer 1997a, p.1)

At the same time, other critics were signalling that Dearing's thinking on higher education was rooted in an outmoded model and should not be seen in isolation from the debate about the funding of lifelong learning:

> Much of its thinking remains rooted in the idea that real higher education is what happens to people in late adolescence. In the short term its funding recommendations do not tackle the most significant inequity, that between students in further and higher education. (Tuckett 1997, p.1)

The short time between the publication of the Kennedy Report on widening participation in further education and the Dearing Report on the purposes, shape, structure, size and funding of higher education, served to focus some debate on the related issues of access and participation to post-compulsory education under the banner of lifelong learning, which was beginning to be viewed in terms of a continuum from further to higher education:

> Both the Dearing and Kennedy reports focus our attention on the problem of the social composition of post-school education. If we want to shift to lifelong learning for all, for the many and not the few, as Labour says, we have to correct the problem of the

---

2 Blackstone was reported by Tony Tysome in *THES* 1997b, p.1, to have given assurances to universities that extra money raised by tuition fees would go to higher educaton.

skewed population in colleges and universities. (Fryer 1997b, p.1)

Reactions to the Dearing Report were mixed. The *THES*, in an article titled 'Lifelong learning left on fringe', reports NIACE's view that the Dearing Report, in its proposals on student funding, 'seriously fails to recognise the lifelong learning agenda' (*THES* 1997c, p.4); the Society of Research into Higher Education view that the Dearing report lacks a 'strong and coherent vision of the learning society of the future' (p.4); the Council for Industry and Higher Education view that the report 'did not go far enough in placing higher education firmly as part of a lifelong learning system' (p.4); whilst the FEFC argued that 'it does not consider restricting institutions in further and higher education to distinctive qualifications will sufficiently encourage lifelong learning' (p.4). The lobby group for the 1992 universities took a similar view and argued that 'The wholesale transfer of [sub-degree] courses to FE colleges would be a devastating blow to the new universities and would send the wrong signals on the importance of professional and vocational higher education' (Coalition of Modern Universities 1997, p.7). On the other hand, NATFHE 'welcomed the approach by Dearing, that the aim of higher education should be "to sustain a learning society"' (NATFHE 1997, p.1).

One of the more predictable consequences of the introduction of tuition fees for undergraduate study was that some universities would break ranks and decide to waive tuition fees. In a move roundly condemned by its neighbouring competitors, the University of Central England in Birmingham announced in December 1997 that it would waive tuition fees for students applying for 1998–9 entry to certain programmes in the faculty of engineering and computer technology and the faculty of the built environment. This was against the background of an expected drop in overall student applications following the government announcement on tuition fees, and 'in response to a large dip in applications to read the two subjects' (*THES* 1997d, p.1). The spectre of a developing market between providers of full-time undergraduate programmes in which there is competition on price discounting and financial incentives to students appears to be moving ever closer. Competition on price will lead to increased expenditure on marketing, further downward pressure on unit costs leading to further trimming of provision, inevitably giving rise to further concerns within quality agencies and others about academic standards and quality assurance, thus increasing the likelihood of even more centralised control over curriculum and quality audit. This nightmare scenario is a present reality in the further education sector and, as in that sector, the strategy of commodification of formal education is consistent with the inherent government aim of introducing greater political control whilst ensuring year-on-year cost savings. Higher education institutions have more to lose than academic freedom by playing at big business.

The Dearing Report has little to offer for part-time students who comprise over a third of all students in higher education. Many were looking to the report to eradicate the anomaly under which part-time students are at a financial disadvantage. Whilst it recognises that there is a problem about the funding of part-time students it does little to ameliorate it. It rejects extending loan or grant arrangements to part-time students on the grounds that many part-time students have their fees paid by their employer, that a high proportion are in employment and therefore able to support themselves, and that to do so would involve high costs. A means tested loans system is ruled out on the grounds of administration costs. The report does recommend that government enable institutions to waive tuition fees for part time students in receipt of jobseekers allowance or certain family benefits, ensuring that within the benefits system there are no financial disincentives to part-time study by the unemployed or those on low incomes, and extending eligibility for access fund payments to part-time students. Part of the difficulty on funding part-time students is that many are studying by distance learning, some eight per cent with the Open University, and government would not wish to make funding available to them. Of part-time students following traditionally taught courses, those whose fees are paid by their employer are in the main following professional or vocational courses; the majority who are studying undergraduate and postgraduate courses do not fall into this category, and under Dearing's proposals will continue to be marginalised; in short the report does not 'ensure that all adults are able to secure access to learning opportunities on equal terms ... We should stop paying lip-service to lifelong learning and do something about it' (Daniel 1997, p.8). Perhaps more fundamentally however, the report perpetuates a major myth about making any distinction between part-time and full-time students on the grounds of employment. The reality is that a large proportion of full-time students are employed in paid work, and many have more than one job.

From the point of view of practitioners, the sharpest criticism of the report is that which has been directed at its mischaracterisation of what higher education is about. Recalling similar comments by Martin Trow (see Preface) Fergus Millar takes Dearing to task for the way in which the report is 'written in complete obliviousness both of the professional roles of contemporary academics and of the essential character of both teaching and research in universities: that they do not deliver unproblematic lumps of "skills" or "information"; but are concerned with method, principles and a critical approach to what is claimed to be true' (Millar 1997, p.11).

There is a real danger that the most telling epitaph for the Dearing Report is that provided by Gordon Lapping, Professor of Communication and Media Studies at the University of Poppleton:

> Although Sir Ron's report may be remembered less for its own sake and more for the opportunity it provided for the government to do what it wanted in the first place, it is nevertheless a very long and heavy document and clearly shows what can be achieved when a very large number of important people get together for fourteen months. (Taylor 1997, p.9)

It is perhaps an unfair criticism that governments now seem unable to make a decision on education without commissioning a report or a review. However there are real difficulties with this approach. First, as illustrated by the government response on tuition fees to the National Committee of Inquiry on Higher Education, the exercise is to some extent pointless, since government is under no obligation to accept or implement recommendations generated by these documents. Second, the terms of reference are inevitably set broadly, but any breadth of vision which they contain is rapidly narrowed and diluted by economic imperatives. Third there is a certain madness in commissioning a number of reports which inevitably overlap each other, might complement each other, but more likely simply serve to diffuse any sharp focus on real issues. It is preposterous that separate reports on widening participation in further education, the structure and funding of higher education and continuing education and lifelong learning could appear within months of each other. What is the logic of that? Behind the rhetoric of ensuring 'transparent links and pathways between different forms and levels of learning provision' (NAGCELL 1997, p.72), where is the lead from government? If the government's own approach is demonstrably fragmented and arcanely conservative, what hope for policies that might enact lifelong learning? This fragmentation is at least recognised in Fryer's comments on the quality assurance of lifelong learning:

> Much of the pressure in quality assurance work in recent years has focused on the identification and monitoring of planned, and quantifiable outcomes from learning programmes. To some extent, this has privileged predicted learning outcomes over those revealed, learned in the process, and has focused on the short-term and easily measured rather than longer-term measures, and those involving qualitative judgement. It has also centred on individual as against group learning.

> Changes in the pattern of work have posed challenges to auditors, in the audit of non-waged work and its conribution to the national economy. A similar challenge exists for educators, and the quality assurance agencies, to develop rigorous audit tools that better reflect the complexity of 'learning gain' in lifelong learning. This task would be helped if the inspectorates currently working for OFSTED, FEFC, the new Training Inspectorate and the Quality Assurance Agency for Higher Education could harmonise their approach to inspection, establishing common methods, criteria and perspectives in inspection. Inspection staff could either conduct joint enquiries or work in discrete arenas, but within a broadly common framework, increasingly sharing their experience and the outcomes of their work. (NAGCELL 1997, p.80)

At the heart, however, of the problem is the restricted vision which is now applied by the government to education. The adoption by New Labour of Conservative market policies, and the decision to remain within Conservative spending plans for the first two years of government, demonstrate the constricted arena within which the lifelong learning agenda can be played out:

> If New Labour is to avoid the parochial nation state response of the New Right, it will need to publicly acknowledge what it is up against, and tackle the policy consequences head on. The mistake for Labour is to imagine that it can harness market forces

to its advantage in a similar, but different way, to the New Right. Perhaps the real problem is that Labour, constrained by a lack of vision of the alternatives, has come to believe that there are no real alternatives ...What is lacking in both the political and academic domain is any serious attempt to critically examine why public policy is the way it is, and 'to theorise the conditions for a different form of polity and public policy' (Ranson 1995) ... [T]his would seem important since the combination of market and managerialist policies fragments what students, practitioners and institutions learn and do, and the possibility of their seeking common purpose.' (Gleeson 1996, p.524)

There is no doubt that lifelong learning has been adopted as a banner project by the government; this can be demonstrated by reference to the DfEE world wide web homepage, from where at the time of writing a link is provided to a new DfEE-sponsored lifelong learning website where the following text is available:

Adult Further Education

Learning doesn't stop when you leave school or college. These days two-thirds of further education students are adults. Many study full or part time at further education colleges for qualifications to help them gain employment or progress in their careers. Others, especially older people, follow leisure or recreational courses, with no firm goal in mind beyond the enjoyment of learning.

The Further Education Funding Councils (one each for England and Wales) and local education authorities (LEAs) are together responsible legally for securing adequate further education for adults. The Government too is fully committed to all kinds of adult learning and has ensured that both the FEFCs and LEAs are funded to meet all their statutory duties.

(www.lifelonglearning.co.uk/adult/further.htm Accessed 10.12.97)

There are two major difficulties here. The first is that whilst the government is enthusiastic about lifelong learning, it still does not acknowledge its responsibility to bring it about. In the above extract, government is seen as only one player among several with its commitment limited to fulfilling its statutory responsibilities. There is little sense of leading, let alone expanding, opening out, fostering, nurturing, enlivening or celebrating learning and learners. The problem with the adoption by the government of lifelong learning as a policy theme is that is has been parent to a good deal of empty rhetoric. In a highly critical report by the director of the ESRC's £2 million learning society programme, Frank Coffield, the ideology of human capital is exposed for what it is – 'a comforting ideology which deflects attention away from the structural causes of poverty onto individuals' (Coffield 1997, p.4) and the ideology of lifelong learning itself is exposed as 'a set of worthy propositions which claim that "learning pays", "learning empowers" and "learning civilises" and so on. It is the safe, middle class view of learning, propounded by those who have succeeded in our formerly elite system of education and whose learning has indeed paid off handsomely for them (p.3).

In tune with much of the thinking of New Labour, its proposals on lifelong learning are designed to smother the idea in an apolitical discourse, seeking in the process to transfer some of the burden of education and training costs to the individual learner – in effect translating an entitlement into a commodity. Within the further education sector voucher schemes, where the learner is given vouchers (like a chequebook) to purchase (usually) occupation-specific training, have proved popular with employers. Such schemes have been characterised as underpinned by a means-end conception of the educational process which is intellectually dubious and epistemologically threadbare (Hyland 1992). However, such approaches seem to be gaining ground, and have found a new lease of life in the proposals for Individual Learning Accounts (ILAs) (NCIHE 1997, p.344; FEFC 1997b, p.74), which are nothing more than voucher schemes by another name, as the following characteristics identified in the Dearing Report make clear. Paragraph 18 of Report 13 (of the NCIHE) defines an ILA as:

- an accumulation fund: providing opportunities for investment by allowing individuals, their families, the state and/or employers to deposit cash sums into the ILA with a view to accumulating funds for the purchase of lifelong learning and to meet the repayment of outstanding loans and overdrafts;

- a distribution fund: providing a facility for individual discretionary control of funds by permitting individual access to, and control over, the distribution funds with the account, circumscribed by the purchase limitations and other rules governing the account;

- a loan/overdraft facility: allowing individual access to loans from public or private sources with which to meet the costs of tuition fees and/or personal maintenance when pursuing a course or learning opportunities;

- a repayment mechanism: providing for secure and equitable repayment of loans, debts, overdrafts and so forth. (NCIHE 1997, p.344)

This development can be seen as part of the process of individualisation of learning that privatises education and draws attention away from the communal and social aspects of learning. Learning accounts are promoted using the discourse which implies that education is valued and has a value, requiring investment from a number of stakeholders including the learner, the employer and government. This discourse is very reminiscent of Freire's (1972) banking model of education in which learning is seem as something that is passed on from teacher to student, as in an economic transaction within the marketplace. As Jansen and Wildemeersch (1996) have pointed out: 'The thesis of individualization may create the wrong impression that, in today's society, people can autonomously shape their own identity development [which] distracts attention from the fact that identity development is a continuous project carried out *in interaction between the individual and contradictory social relations*' (1996, p.328, original italics). Such a development is a good example of the way in which the world of adult education has increasingly become characterised by increasing 'economising' (Kenway 1994) and accountability of its systems (Power 1994), performativity of its practitioners (Lyotard 1979) and where even knowledge itself becomes an object of consumption (Edwards and Usher 1996).

I want to end by suggesting that the benefits of the present policy focus on lifelong learning have yet to be realised. The initiatives and developments reported and commented upon in this book are viewed within a socio-political perspective, less significant for the schemes which they initiate than for the extent to which they are an early articulation of a new policy agenda for education. That is not to deny that some of these developments do not have the potential to be effective in widening participation or bringing about improvements in effective learning. However, the broader significance is that there is an emerging discourse of individual empowerment and agency. Ironically that was initiated by the previous Conservative government, but used by them to develop an individualised and mechanistic policy direction with a wholesale emphasis on accountancy and audit leading to a series of education reforms including the establishment of the NCVQ, OFSTED, and the funding and quality regimes governing further and higher education. Within that era the individual's claim on education was as a customer or shareholder, bringing the expectations of a consumer of a branded product who would receive value for money within a competitive education service that was required to meet quantitative performance indicators. The problem with that system is that, contrary to the illusion and the rhetoric of the discourse, it closes down individual choices and agency. As recognised in the Kennedy Report (FEFC 1997), the market has failed in widening participation.

What is needed is a cross-sector approach. Piecemeal reform will not do. As West argues, writing about the schools sector, the task is to establish a locally accountable democratic education policy:

> the problems of modern society can only be resolved by the fostering of new civic partnerships: the involvement of education's stakeholders. The political voice and skills of governing bodies and local communities are important elements in this: the only elements at present perhaps that can lift schools out of the sterile concentration of administration and technique: there is in other words a need for the concept of self-management to extend to that of self-governance and co-governance, for without political voice and participation, at the local level the skills of government could so easily be replaced by a tier of technocrats – the accessories of hegemony. We have to begin again in building the democratic process and in unearthing civic awareness from traditional assumptions, paternalism and market silences. (West 1996, p.92)

The difficulty is that if the world is one that is characterised by postmodern fragmentation, where is the capacity for values such as participative democracy to be shared? One way forward is to adopt an approach which recognises, values and constitutes fracture by 'developing the capacities of citizens to engage in the remaking of their societies in a postmodern world of difference' (Ranson 1998).

Whether such a project can be achieved is unknown, but it may be that a constitutive discourse of lifelong learning can be effective in shaping an agenda that consigns impoverished, market-based consumerist education policies to the dustbin of history. Which wouldn't be a bad start towards bringing about a society of lifelong learning.

References

Allan, J. (1996) Learning Outcomes in Higher Education. *Studies in Higher Education 21*, 1, 93–108.

Association of Colleges (1997) Letter headed 'Demand Led Element', dated 27 January 1997, sent to Corporation Chairs and Chief Executives.

Argyris, C. and Schon, D. (1978) *Organisational Learning Theory*. New York: Addison Wesley.

Avis, J. (1997) 'Leftist ethnography, educative research and post-compulsory education and training.' *Research in Post-Compulsory Education 2*, 1, 5–15.

Barnett, R. (1994) *The Limits of Competence*. Buckingham: SRHE/Open University Press.

Barnett R. (1996) 'Being and becoming: a student trajectory.' *International Journal of Lifelong Education 15*, 2 72–84.

Barnett, R. (1997) 'A knowledge strategy for universities.' In R. Barnett and A. Griffin (eds) *The End of Knowledge in Higher Education*. Institute of Education Series. London: Cassell.

Barnett, R. and Griffin, A. (eds) *The End of Knowledge in Higher Education*. Institute of Education Series. London: Cassell.

Bateson, G. (1973) *Steps to an Ecology of Mind*. New York: Paladin.

Beasley, J. (1996) 'From dropout to doormouse: a study of Access route discontinuation in HE.' *Access Networking 2*, 7.

Bengtsson, J. (1979) 'The work/leisure/education life cycle.' In *World Yearbook of Education 1979*. London: Kogan Page.

Benn, R. and Burton, R. (1995) 'Access and targeting: an exploration of a contradiction.' *International Journal of Lifelong Education 14*, 6, 444–458.

Berger, T. (1967) *A Way of Seeing*. Harmondsworth: Penguin.

Biggs, J. (1989) 'Does learning about learning help teachers with teaching? Psychology and the tertiary teacher.' *The Gazette 26* (Supplement), 1, University of Hong Kong (cited in G. Gibbs, 1992, 155–6).

Biggs, J. (1993) 'From theory to practice: a cognitive systems approach,' *Higher Education Research and Development 12*, 73–85.

Biggs, J. and Collis, K. (1982) *Evaluating the Quality of Learning: the Solo Taxonomy*. New York: Academic Press.

Blackstone, T. (1997a) In G. Goodman (ed) *The State of the Nation: the Politics and Legacy of Aneurin Bevan*. Extracts in *THES* 17 October, 22.

Blackstone, T. (1997b) Quoted in T. Tysome 'Students stitch up Ron.' *THES* 25 July, 1.

Bloland, G. (1997) 'The critical paradigm.' http://www.it.stedwards.edu/newc/kilgore/critical.htm Accessed 22.07.97.

Bowles, S. and Gintis, H. (1976) *Schooling in Capitalist Americaz*. London: Routledge and Kegan Paul.

Boyle, C. (1982) 'Reflections on recurrent education.' *International Journal of Lifelong Learning 1*, 1, 5–18.

Brookfield, S. (1986) *Understanding and Facilitating Adult Learning*. Milton Keynes: Open University Press.

Caldwell, B. (1997) 'The future of public education: a policy framework for lasting reform.' *Educational Management and Adminstration 25*, 4, 357–370.

Campaign for Learning (1997) *Learning to Live*. Newsletter, 4.

Claxton, G. (1996) 'Implicit theories of learning.' In G. Claxton, T. Atkinson, M. Osborn and M. Wallace (eds) *Liberating the Learner: Lessons for Professional Development in Education*. London: Routledge.

Coalition of Modern Universities (1997) Response to the Dearing Report, quoted in 'Mission drift in sub-degree sea,' *THES* 10 October, 7.

Coare, P. and Thomson, A. (1996) *Through the Joy of Learning: Diary of 1,000 Adult Learners*. Leicester: NIACE.

Coffield, F. (1997) *A National Strategy for Lifelong Learning*. Newcastle: University of Newcastle.

Corrigan, P. (1979) *Schooling the Smash Street Kids*. London: Macmillan.

Daniel, J. (1997) Quoted in 'First reactions', *THES* 25 July, 8.

Dave, R. (ed.) (1976) *Foundations of Lifelong Learning*. Oxford: Pergamon.

Dawe, R. (1997) Letter to David Melville, Chief Executive of the FEFC, dated 20 January 1997, from Roger Dawe, Director General for Further and Higher Education and Youth Training, DfEE.

Dearing, R. (1997) Quoted in H. Swain 'Fees: there's no limit', *THES* 1 August, 3.

Department for Education and Employment (1996) *Lifetime Learning: a Policy Framework*. London: DfEE.

Department for Education and Employment (1997) Briefing Paper: *Getting the Most out of HE – Supporting Learner Autonomy*. London: DfEE.

Derrida, J. (1976) *Of Grammatology*. Baltimore: Johns Hopkins University Press.

Dewey, J. (1916) *Democracy and Education: an Introduction to the Philosophy of Education*. New York: Macmillan.

Duke, C. (1982) 'Evolution of the recurrent education concept.' *International Journal of Lifelong Education 1*, 4, 323–340.

Edwards, R. and Usher, R. (1996) 'What stories do I tell now? New times and new narratives for the adult educator.' *International Journal of Lifelong Education 15*, 3, 216–229.

Elliott, G. (1994) 'Why is research invisible in further education?' *British Educational Research Journal 22*, 1, 101–111.

Elliott, G. (1996) *Crisis and Change in Vocational Education and Training*. London: Jessica Kingsley.

Elliott, G. and Crossley, M. (1994) 'Qualitative research, educational management and the incorporation of the further education sector.' *Educational Management and Administration 22*, 3, 188–197.

Fieldhouse, R. (1996) 'Mythmaking and mortmain: a response.' *Studies in the Education of Adults 28*, 1 (cited in Coare and Thomson, 1996, 201).

Foucault, M. (1979a) *Discipline and Punish: The Birth of the Prison.* London: Penguin.

Foucault, M. (1979b) *History of Sexuality, Vol. 1.* London: Allen Lane.

Freire, P. (1972) *Pedagogy of the Oppressed,* trans. Myra Bergman Rumos. Harmondsworth: Penguin.

Fryer, B. (1994) 'The core values of adult education.' *Education Today and Tomorrow 46*, 2, 18–19.

Fryer, R. (1997a) Quoted in P. Baty, A. Thomson and H. Swain 'Dearing snubbed by policy drafters' *THES* 1 August, 1.

Fryer, R. (1997b) Quoted in 'FE revolution for universities' *THES* 10 October, 1.

Further Education Funding Council (1996a) *Learning and Technology Committee Report.* Coventry: FEFC the Higginson Committee.

Further Education Funding Council (1996b) *Pathways to Success: the Widening Participation Committee Emerging Conclusions.* Coventry: FEFC.

Further Education Funding Council (1997a) *Chief Inspector's Annual report: Quality and Standards in Further Education in England 1996–7.* Coventry: FEFC.

Further Education Funding Council (1997b) *Learning Works: Widening Particpation in Further Education* (The Kennedy Report). Coventry: FEFC.

Further Education Funding Council (1997c) Press release headed 'Cash Threat to Colleges', dated 27 January. Coventry: FEFC.

Garratt, B. (1990) *Creating a Learning Organisation: a Guide to Leadership, Learning and Development.* Cambridge: Director Books, in association with the Institute of Directors.

Gibbs, G. (1992) 'Improving the quality of student learning through course design.' In R. Barnett (ed) (1992) *Learning to Effect.* Buckingham: SRHE Open University Press.

Glaser, B. and Strauss, A. (1965) 'The discovery of substantive theory: a basic strategy underlying qualitative research.' *American Behavioral Scientist, 8*, 6, 5–12.

Glaser, B. and Strauss, A. (1967) *The Discovery of Grounded Theory.* Chicago: Aldine.

Gleeson, D. (1996) 'In the public interest: post-compulsory education in a postmodern age.' *Journal of Education Policy 11*, 5, 513–26.

Gorard, S., Rees, G., Fevre, R. and Furlong, J. (1997) Learning Trajectories: Travelling Towards a Learning Society? Paper given at BERA Conference, University of York.

Gouldner, A. (1970) *The Coming Crisis of Western Sociology.* New York: Basic Books.

Griffin, C. (1978) *Recurrent and Continuing Education – a Curriculum Approach.* Association for Recurrent Education, Discussion paper No. 3 (cited in Boyle,1982).

Griffin, C. (1982) 'Curriculum analysis of adult and lifelong learning.' *International Journal of Lifelong Learning 1*, 2, 109–121.

Griffiths, D. (1997) 'The case for theoretical pluralism.' *Educational Management and Administration 25*, 4, 371–80.

Habermas, J. (1984) *Theory of Communicative Action, Vol. 1.* Cambridge: Polity Press.

Hallinger, P. (1997) 'Taking charge of change'. *International Studies in Educational Administration 25*, 1 , 27–34.

Hargreaves, A. (1991) 'Contrived collegiality.' In J. Blase *The Politics of Life in Schools.* Newbury Park, CA: Sage Publications.

Hodkinson, P. and Sparkes, A. (1995) 'Markets and vouchers: the inadequacy of individualist policies for vocational education and training in Englsnd and Wales.' *Journal of Education Policy 10*, 2, 189–207.

Houghton, V. and Richardson, K. (eds) (1974) *Recurrent Education: a Plea for Lifelong Learning.* London: Ward Lock.

Hyland, T. (1992) 'The vicissitudes of adult education: competence, epistemology and reflective practice.' *Education Today 42*, 2, 7–12.

Hyland, T. (1994) 'Silk purses and sows ears: NVQs, GNVQs and experiential learning.' *Cambridge Journal of Education 24* 2, 233–243.

Innis, K. and Shaw, M. (1997) 'How do students spennd their time?' *Quality Assurance in Education 5*, 2, 85–89.

Jansen, T. and Wildemeersch, D. (1996) 'Adult education and vcritical identity development: from a deficiency orientation towards a competency orientation.' *International Journal of Lifelong Education 15*, 5, 325–340.

Kenway, J. (1994) *Economising Education: the Post-Fordist Direction.* Deakin: Deakin University Press.

King, E. (1977) 'Education for a communications dociety.' In E. King (ed) *Reorganizing Education: Management and Participation for Change*, Sage Annual Review of Social and Educational Change. London: Sage Publications.

Knowles, M. (1980) *The Modern Practice of Adult Education: from Pedagogy to Andragogy* 2nd edn. New York: Cambridge Books.

Laurillard, D. (1993) *Rethinking University Teaching: a Framework for the Effective Use of Information Technology.* London: Routledge.

Lawson K (1982) 'Lifelong education: concept or policy?' *International Journal of Lifelong Education 1*, 2, 97–108.

Longworth, N. and Davies, W. (1996) *Lifelong Learning.* London: Kogan Page.

Lyotard, J. (1979) *The Post-modern Condition: a Report on Knowledge.* Manchester: Manchester University Press.

McCracken, G. (1988) *The Long Interview.* Newbury Park CA: Sage Publications.

McIlroy, J. (1994) 'Access pedagogy and changing higher education.' *Adults Learning 6*, 3, November, 97.

McKenzie, J. and Scott, G. (1993) 'Teachng Matters: making a video on teaching in higher education.' *Research and Development in Higher Education 16*, 419–424.

McNair, S. (1997) 'Is there a crisis? Does it Matter?' In R. Barnett and A. Griffin (eds) *The End of Knowledge in Higher Education*. London: Cassell

Malinowski, B. (1922) *Argonauts of the Western Pacific*. London: Routledge and Kegan Paul.

Millar, F. (1997) 'Open pursuit of knowledge.' *THES* 12 September 12, 11.

National Advisory Group for Continuing Education and Lifelong Learning (1997) *Learning for the Twenty-First Century: First report of the National Advisor Group for Continuing Education and Lifelong Learning* (The Fryer Report). NAGCELL.

National Association of Teachers in Further and Higher Education (1997) 'Dearing: pros and cons.' *HE News*, October, 1.

National Committee of Inquiry into Higher Education (1997) *Higher Education in the Learning Society* The Dearing Report. London: HMSO.

National Institute for Adult Continuing Education (1997) *Annual Report and Accounts 1996–7*. Leicester: NIACE.

O'Neill, J. (1972) *Sociology as a Skin Trade: Essays Towards a Reflexive Sociology*. London: Heinemann.

Organisation for Economic Cooperation and Development (1973) *Recurrent Education: a Strategy for Lifelong Learning. Paris: OECD.*

Pedler, M., Burgoyne, J. and Boydell, T. (1991) *The Learning Company*. London: McGraw Hill.

Peters, T. (1989) *Thriving on Chaos: Handbook for a Management Revolution*. London: Pan/Macmillan.

Peters, T. and Waterman, R. (1982) *In Search of Excellence: Lessons from America's Best-Run Companies*. New York: Harper and Row.

Power, M. (1994) *The Audit Explosion*. London: Demos.

Ramsden, P. (1992) *Learning to Teach in Higher Education*. London: Routledge.

Ranson, S. (1995) 'Theorising education policy.' *British Journal of Education Policy 10*, 4, 427–448.

Ranson, S. (1998) Lecture given in Faculty of Education Evening Lecture Series, University of Central England in Birmingham, 22 January.

Richardson, J. (1994) 'Mature students in higher education: I. A literature survey on approaches to studying.' *Studies in Higher Education 19*, 3, 309–325.

Richardson, J. (1995) 'Mature Students in Higher Education: II. An investigation of approaches to studying and academic performance.' *Studies in Higher Education 20*, 1, 5–17.

Richardson, J. (1997) 'Dispelling some myths about mature students in higher education: study skills, approaches to studying, and intellectual ability.' In P Sutherland (ed) *Adult Learning: A Reader*. London: Kogan Page.

Robbins Committee (1962) *Higher Education*. London: HMSO.

Robertson, D. (1993) 'Flexibility and mobility in further and higher education: policy continuity and progress.' *Journal of Further and Higher Education 17*. 1, 68–79.

Rowan, J. (1981) 'A dialectical paradigm for research.' In P. Reason and J. Rowan (eds) *Human Inquiry.* New York: John Wiley.

Shah, S. (1994) 'Kaleidoscope people: locating the "subject" of pedagogic discourse.' *Journal of Access Studies 9,* 2, 257–270.

Schratz, M. (1995) *Research as Social Change: New Opportunities for Qualitative Research.* London: Routledge.

Smith, N. and Taylor, P. (1997) Scottish Low Pay Unit Study of Student Part-Time Working, reported in *THES* 17 October, 4.

Smith, R. and Havercamp, K. (1977) 'Toward a theory of learning how to learn.' *Adult Education (USA) 28,* 1, 3–21.

Stenhouse, L. (1979) 'Case study in comparative education: particularity and generalisation.' *Comparative Education 15,* 1, 5–11.

Stenhouse, L. (1980) *Curriculum Research and Development in Action.* London: Heinemann.

Swain, H. 'Fees: there's no limit' *THES* 1 August, 3.

Taylor, L. (1997) Column in *THES* 25 July, 9.

The Times Educational Supplement (1997) 'Principals furious at funding freeze.' 31 January, 1.

The Times Higher Educational Supplement (1997a) 'Gates pleads the case for good teachers.' 10 October, 2.

The Times Higher Educational Supplement (1997b) 'Students stitch up Ron.' 25 July, 1.

The Times Higher Educational Supplement (1997c) 'Lifelong Learning left on the fringe.' 17 October, 4.

The Times Higher Educational Supplement (1997d) 'Flexible fees inevitable.' *THES* 12 December, 1.

Trigwell, K. and Prosser, M. (1996) 'Changing approches to Teaching: a relational approach.' *Studies in Higher Education 21,* 3, 275–284.

Trow, M. (1997) 'More trouble than it's worth.' *THES* 24 October, 26.

Trowler, P. (1997) 'Beyond the Robbins trap: reconceptualising academic responses to change in higher education (or... Quiet Flows the Don?)' *Studies in Higher Education 22,* 3, 301–318.

Trueman, M. and Hartley, J. (1996) 'A comparison between the time-management skills and academic performance of mature and traditional entry university students.' *Higher Education 32,* 199–215.

Tuckett, A. (1997) Quoted in P. Baty, A. Thomson and H. Swain 'Dearing snubbed by policy drafters.' *THES* 1 August, 1.

Tysome, T. (1997) 'Personal savings bank for learning.' *THES* 10 October, 3.

Waldrop, M. (1992) *Complexity.* New York: Simon and Schuster.

West, S. (1996) 'Competition and collaboration in education: marriage not divorce.' In D. Bridges and C. Husbands (eds) *Consorting and Collaborating in the Education Marketplace.* London: The Falmer Press.

Whitehead, A. (1932) *The Aims of Education and Other Essays.* (cited in P. Broadfoot (1981) 'The impact of research on educational studies', *British Journal of Educational Studies 29*, 2, 115–122.

Willis, P. (1977) *Learning to Labour: How Working Class Kids get Working Class Jobs.* Farnborough, Hants: Saxon House.

Woodley, A. (1981) 'Age bias.' In D. Warren Piper (ed) *Is Higher Education Fair?* Guildford: Society for Research into Higher Education (cited in Richardson, 1994, 309).

Wrong, D. (1961) 'The conception of man.' *American Sociological Review 26.*

Subject Index

andragogy, 39–40, 42
Association of Colleges, 120
Campaign for Learning, 93
Central England, University of, 123
Centre for Educational Research and Innovation, 32
Coalition of Modern Universities, 123
competition in further education, *see* further education; adoption of market principles
complexity theory, *see* education, complexity theory in
continuing education and lifelong learning, 83–85
Council for Industry and Higher Education, 123
credit systems, 34–36
Dearing Report (1997), 7–8, 17, 98–104, 120–127
Department for Education and Employment, *Getting the Most Out of Higher Education* (1997), 10
Department for Education and Employment, *Lifetime Learning,* 31
duetero-learning, 11

discourse analysis methods, 22–23
education, American post-secondary system of, 33–34
complexity theory in, 20–21
formal, 29–33, 38, 79–85
post-compulsory, 17–19, 24–27, 61, 79–92
recurrent, 83–85
research in, 79–92
educational policy, its failures, 7–8, 12, 24–26, 74, 112–115
European Lifelong Learning Initiative, 25–26
Fryer Report (1997), 17, 104–109, 122–126
further and higher education, boundaries, 17–18
further education, adoption of market principles, 112–115, 126–127
co-operation with outside agencies, 113–118
Further Education Development Agency, 80
Further Education Funding Council, 9–10, 119–120
Learning and Technology Committee Report (1996), *see* the Higginson Committee

Learning Works (1997), *see* the Kennedy Report
Pathways to Success, *see* the Kennedy Report
Further Education Research Association, 80
Getting the Most Out of Higher Education (DfEE, 1997), 10
Higginson Committee Report (1996), 9–10
Higher Education in the Learning Society, *see* the Dearing Report
Individual Learning Accounts, 128–9
information technology, its role, 8–10, 14–15
inspectorates, 126
Kennedy Report (1997), 93–98, 112–116, 118
knowledge, practical and technical, 19–21
learning and qualifications, 73
Learning and Technology Committee Report (1996), *see* the Higginson Committee
Learning for the Twenty-First Century, *see* the Fryer Report
Learning Regeneration Fund, 115
Learning Works, *see* the Kennedy Report
lectures, role of, 13, 73–75
lifelong learning, 83–85 *see also* the Fryer Report

and continuing
education
requirements,
25–28, 31–34,
37–39
*Lifetime Learning: A Policy
Framework* (DfEE,
1996), 31

National Advisory Group
for Continuing
Education and
Lifelong Learning,
73, 125–126
National Association of
Teachers in Further
and Higher
Education, 123
National Committee of
Enquiry into Higher
Education (1997), *see*
the Dearing Report
National Institute for
Adult Continuing
Education, 10
Northern Lights, 116–118

Organisation for
Economic
Co-operation and
Development, 32

Pathways to Success, *see*
the Kennedy Report
postmodernism in
education, 80–82

recurrent education, *see*
lifelong learning
research in education, *see*
education, research in

Society of Research into
Higher Education,
123
students, approach to
learning, 40–45
development, 11–12,
71–75

influence of course and
college, 47–61
learning process, 12,
23–24, 63–68,
75–77
learning to learn, 10–14
levels of analysis, 76–77
motivation, 68–71, 74
part-time, 124
tuition fees means
tested, 121–124

technology, information
and knowledge,
14–15
tuition fees means tested,
see students, tuition
fees means tested

Wideing Participation
Committee, *see* the
Kennedy Report

Author Index

Allan, J. 13–14
Argyris, C. and Schon, D. 11, 30
Avis, J. 38

Barnett, R. 23–24, 35, 82
Barnett, R. and Griffin, A. 37
Beasley, J. 36–37
Bengtsson, J. 32
Benn, R. and Burton, R. 84
Berger, T. 82
Biggs, J. 12, 74–75
Biggs, J. and Collis, K. 42–43
Blackstone, T. 29, 121–122
Bloland, G. 21
Blunkett, D. 120–121
Bowles, S. and Gintis, H. 79
Boydell, T. see Pedler, M., Burgoyne, J. and Boydell, T.
Boyle, C. 29
Brookfield, S. 11, 14, 23, 39
Burgoyne, J. see Pedler, M., Burgoyne, J. and Boydell, T.
Burton, R. see Benn, R. and Burton, R.

Caldwell, B. 15
Claxton, G. 23, 42–44
Coare, P. and Thomson, A. 84
Coffield, F. 128
Collis, K. see Biggs, J. and Collis, K.
Corrigan, P. 79

Crossley, M. see Elliott, G. and Crossley, M.
Daniel, J. 124
Dave, R. 32
Davies, W. see Longworth, N. and Davies, W.
Dawe, R. 119
Derrida, J. 81
Dewey, J. 32
Duke, C. 26–27, 32

Edwards, R. and Usher, R. 129
Elliott, G. and Crossley, M. 113

Fieldhouse, R. 81, 88
Foucault, M. 81, 88
Freire, P. 21–22, 129
Fryer, B. 17, 22

Garratt, B. 30
Gates, B. 8–9
Gibbs, G. 12, 42–43, 74
Gintis, H. see Bowles, S. and Gintis, H.
Glaser, B. and Strauss, A. 86
Gleeson, D. 127
Gorard, S. 38
Gouldner, A. 82
Griffin, A. 38
  see also Barnett, R. and Griffin, A.
Griffiths, D. 20

Habermas, J. 19
Hallinger, P. 111
Hargreaves, A. 30
Hartley, J. see Trueman, M. and Hartley, J.
Havercamp, K. see Smith, R. and Havercamp, K.
Hodkinson, P. and Sparkes, A. 14
Houghton, V. and Richardson, K. 27
Hyland, T. 14, 128

Innis, K. and Shaw, M. 40
Jansen, T. and Wildemeersch, D. 129

Kennedy, H. 17
Kenway, J. 129
King, E. 32–33, 37
Knowles, M. 39, 42

Lapping, G. 125
Laurillard, D. 11–13
Lawson, K. 38
Longworth, N. and Davies, W. 25
Lyotard, J. 129

McCracken, G. 86
McIlroy, J. 11–12
McKenzie, J. and Scott, G. 42
McNair, S. 37–38
Malinowski, B. 82
Millar, F. 125

O'Neill, J. 82

Pedler, M., Burgoyne, J. and Boydell, T. 30
Peters, T. 111
Peters, T. and Waterman, R. 111
Power, M. 129
Prosser, M. see Trigwell, K. and Prosser, M.

Ramsden, P. 12, 42
Ranson, S. 126–127, 131
Richardson, J. 41–45
Richardson, K. see Houghton, V. and Richardson, K.
Robertson, D. 34
Rowan, J. 86

Schon, D. see Argyris, C. and Schon, D.
Schratz, M. 82, 88
Scott, G. see McKenzie, J. and Scott, G.

Shah, S. 88

Shaw, M. *see* Innis, K. and
  Shaw, M.

Smith, N. and Taylor, P.
  41

Smith, R. and
  Havercamp, K. 11

Sparkes, A. *see*
  Hodkinson, P. and
  Sparkes, A.

Stenhouse, L. 91

Strauss, A. *see* Glaser, B.
  and Strauss, A.

Swain, H. 121–122

Taylor, L. 125

Taylor, P. *see* Smith, N.
  and Taylor, P.

Thomson, A. *see* Coare, P.
  and Thomson, A.

Tomlinson, V. 116

Trigwell, K. and Prosser,
  M. 42

Trow, M. 7–8

Trowler, P. 35–36

Trueman, M. and
  Hartley, J. 44

Tuckett, A. 122

Tysome, T. 18, 121

Usher, R. *see* Edwards, R.
  and Usher, R.

Waldrop, M. 20

Waterman, R. *see* Peters,
  T. and Waterman, R.

West, S. 130

Whitehead, A. 79

Wildemeersch, D. *see*
  Jansen, T. and
  Wildemeersh, D.

Willis, P. 79

Woodley, A. 43

Wrong, D. 35